IMMEDIACY

OUR WAYS OF COPING IN EVERYDAY LIFE

FRED EMIL KATZ

authorHOUSE®

AuthorHouse™
1663 Liberty Drive
Bloomington, IN 47403
www.authorhouse.com
Phone: 1 (800) 839-8640

Published by AuthorHouse   08/12/2016

ISBN: 978-1-5049-7910-8 (sc)
ISBN: 978-1-5049-7909-2 (e)

Books by Fred Emil Katz

Our Quest for Effective Living. Bloomington, IN AuthorHouse, 2015. New edition,
Living in Social Space, forthcoming, 2016.
>An effort to understand the Social Space in which our life is actually lived.

Confronting Evil: Two journeys. Albany, NY SUNY Press, 2004.
>Sequel to the *Ordinary People*...book with return visit to Fred Emil Katz' birthplace.

Ordinary People and Extraordinary Evil. Albany, NY SUNY Press, 1993.
>Routes by which ordinary people can come to participate in social horrors.

Structuralism in Sociology: An Approach to knowledge. Albany, NY SUNY Press, 1976.
>Making knowledge available: from theory to application; from application to theory; obstacles to knowing.

Contemporary Sociological Theory. (Editor) New York: Random House, 1971.

Autonomy and Organization: The Limits of Social Control. New York, Random House, 1968.
>The location and functioning of personal autonomy amid social constraints.

Fred Emil Katz

Essays in Social Systems of Education. Columbia, Mo: University of Missouri, 1965 (Co-author with B. Biddle, et al)

An Approach to Education of Psychiatric Nursing Personnel. New York: National League for Nursing, 1961. (Co-author with G. Lewis and M. J. Holmes)

This book: ***IMMEDIACY: Our ways of coping in Everyday life* --**
    "From the moment of our birth to our last breath, every one of us must cope with the world around us." A social psychology of how this works.

Published, 2016, by AuthorHouse
    1663 Liberty Drive
    Bloomington, IN 47403
    Phone: 1-800-839-8640

Dedication

To three of my teachers at Guilford College who gave me wondrously agitating gifts:

David Stafford, whose own life exemplifies that science and humane concerns can go together,

Frederick Crownfield, who showed me a vision of science—derived from his teacher at Harvard, Alfred North Whitehead—that is passionate in its search for order, irreverent to existing orthodoxy, and disciplined in its focus on a few core issues;

Robert Dinkel, who tantalized me with the idea that alongside practical application of science—in his own life he parlayed science into great commercial success—a stronger science of human behavior need not remain a vague dream. We can help to make it happen.

If the following effort comes somewhere close to their teachings, it will serve a worthy purpose.

Table of Contents

I thank John Wiley & Sons for permission to use an edited version of my paper "Indeterminacy in the Structure of Systems" which appeared in the journal Behavioral Science *(copyright, John Wiley & Sons Limited), and I thank Brain Research Publications, Inc. for permission to use an edited version of my chapter "Bounded Indeterminacy: A Component Part of the Structure of Systems" which appeared in the book,* Collective Phenomena and the Application of Physics to Other Fields of Science, *edited by Norman A. Chigier and Edward A. Stern. In the present book, the section titled "The Unknowable in Immediacy" is an amalgamation of both of these previous publications.*

I also thank the staff of Pentland Press. They were most helpful, competent, and patient in producing the first edition of this book.

Overview:
The Need to Examine Immediacy

From the moment of our birth, every single one of us must cope with the immediate world around oneself. Our survival depends on it. Our happiness depends on it. Our effectiveness as human beings depends on it.

Charles Darwin taught us that species––of plants, of organisms––are in a life-and-death struggle for survival while coping with the immediate circumstances they encounter. Darwin's focus was on the survival process itself, in which the environment––the immediate surroundings––sets the terms of the contest and determines the outcome. The environment carries out the natural selection. It is nature's grand enforcer as to which species will thrive and which will die out.

In Darwin's scenario we focus on large populations––species––rather than individuals. This distracts us from dealing with the actual ongoing life struggles of individual creatures. Yes, species are in survival struggle. But so are individuals. And it is the individual who, invariably, loses the struggle. Each of us dies – but not before a life-long effort to cope with the here and now, in which we actually find ourselves.

Yet Darwin provides the valuable insight that the transaction between an organism and its environment is crucial if one wants to understand how life is lived. In this book I shall dwell on such transaction by humans as individuals. The focus is on the individual social-psychological situation in which transactions take place. This situation is poorly understood, but we can understand it better. Much human pain and suffering is based on needless ignorance about this situation. Our ignorance is not merely the absence of knowledge––of not having enough information––but of inadequate ways of looking at the information we do have. We have to create new ways of looking, so that we may see better.

Many researchers have looked at the social-psychological situation in which humans are living their lives. From the twentieth century, names such as Erving Goffman and Kurt Lewin come to mind. I shall not dwell on the work of these two researchers, except to say that their focus was on how the "field" (in the work of Lewin) impinges on the individual, and how the individual's "self" (in the work of Goffman) is presented to a social context made up of people who evaluate you, and whose judgment you are trying to influence. However I shall quite unabashedly and deliberately make use of work by some researchers from this tradition––notably work by Stanley Milgram and Viktor Frankl––to present a particular point of view of the social immediacy in which humans operate. To do so, I shall change the various researchers' own interpretations of their work.

I shall have us look at social-psychological immediacies as distinct phenomena in their own right. They will be shown to have dimensions that need to be reckoned with when we try to understand how and why people do what they do. I shall examine the following dimensions of immediacy:

1. *Transcendence:* How the structure, pressures, and strains of an immediate situation may be overcome through linkage to a context that goes beyond the immediate one in which individuals find themselves.

2. *Constriction:* In a sense this is the converse of transcendence, namely, how a particular setting in which social behavior takes place can be entirely sealed off from influence by anything outside that setting. As a result of such constriction––especially when it is couched as "moral" constriction––people may do things in one context that they would regard as entirely abhorrent if done in another.

3. *Impingings:* How external and distant elements can intrude into an immediate situation and permeate it, even though the immediate situation has an identity of its own.

4. *Transformation:* How changes can produce new immediacies through a distinctive process. Transformation is viewed in terms of personal life and careers, as well as in a larger, societal dimension.

5. *The unknowable in immediacy:* How some forms of not-knowing are both inevitable in how life is lived and are actually necessary. They are an inherent component part of many sorts of systems.

In the following pages I suggest that immediacy does not merely have distinctive dimensions that make a difference in how people lead their lives. It can have an identity and momentum of its own. Immediacy can be shown to have self-organizing and self-sustaining properties. Finally, I operate from the faith that many of the processes operating in immediacy are patterned and orderly, and can be understood dispassionately.

This point of view, this paradigm, will be developed and illustrated through essays on topics as varied as cults, Adolf Hitler as a false messiah, the famous Milgram experiments on people's willingness to inflict pain on innocent people, a sociology of sexuality, evolution theory, the role of anti-Semitism in fifteenth-century Spain (using Benzion Netanyahu's study) and, finally, an essay on systems theory in which the importance of not knowing (I call it indeterminacy) is explored. Together, these essays illustrate the outward manifestations of immediacy and some of the underlying characteristics––the orderliness––of immediacy. The latter is what really counts if one wants to understand immediacy. The essays explore the paradigm that beneath the fleeting events of immediacy there is an underlying orderliness that revolves around immediacy itself.

The following essays are offered in support of the immediacy paradigm. A paradigm is a venture. Any paradigm must stand or fall on the basis of its capacity to answer one challenge: Does it contribute to our understanding of the world in which we live? I am fully aware that the history of science teaches us a number of lessons about new paradigms.

(1) Each new paradigm requires departure from some existing way of thinking, and yet some individuals will be willing to explore the usefulness of the new paradigm.

(2) Sooner or later the new paradigm will, itself, be supplanted by better ones––paradigms that explain more.

(3) But while it lasts, the new paradigm may add to our understanding of the world around us, as the usefulness of its perspective is being explored. This last item is the incentive for this book.

5. *The unknowable in immediacy:* How some forms of not-knowing are both inevitable in how life is lived and are actually necessary. They are an inherent component part of many sorts of systems.

In the following pages I suggest that immediacy does not merely have distinctive dimensions that make a difference in how people lead their lives. It can have an identity and momentum of its own. Immediacy can be shown to have self-organizing and self-sustaining properties. Finally, I operate from the faith that many of the processes operating in immediacy are patterned and orderly, and can be understood dispassionately.

This point of view, this paradigm, will be developed and illustrated through essays on topics as varied as cults, Adolf Hitler as a false messiah, the famous Milgram experiments on people's willingness to inflict pain on innocent people, a sociology of sexuality, evolution theory, the role of anti-Semitism in fifteenth-century Spain (using Benzion Netanyahu's study) and, finally, an essay on systems theory in which the importance of not knowing (I call it indeterminacy) is explored. Together, these essays illustrate the outward manifestations of immediacy and some of the underlying characteristics––the orderliness––of immediacy. The latter is what really counts if one wants to understand immediacy. The essays explore the paradigm that beneath the fleeting events of immediacy there is an underlying orderliness that revolves around immediacy itself.

The following essays are offered in support of the immediacy paradigm. A paradigm is a venture. Any paradigm must stand or fall on the basis of its capacity to answer one challenge: Does it contribute to our understanding of the world in which we live? I am fully aware that the history of science teaches us a number of lessons about new paradigms.

(1) Each new paradigm requires departure from some existing way of thinking, and yet some individuals will be willing to explore the usefulness of the new paradigm.

(2) Sooner or later the new paradigm will, itself, be supplanted by better ones––paradigms that explain more.

(3) But while it lasts, the new paradigm may add to our understanding of the world around us, as the usefulness of its perspective is being explored. This last item is the incentive for this book.

Ancestry of this Book

Human social behavior sciences have not achieved the level of success and viability as the biological and physical sciences. Is this because human social behavior is inherently more complicated than biological or physical processes? I shall not take time to discuss such an academic issue. Nor shall I list the episodes of ghastly miscalculation and unparalleled brutality that characterized so much of human social behavior during the past century. These remind us all too painfully of the anemic state of the human social behavior sciences in this modern era of science, with its wondrous successes in carving out zones of fruitful control over some aspects of nature. For the human behavior sciences, would new ventures help advance our science?

This book plunges into one such venture. It explores a new paradigm––a new perspective––to see how far it will carry us toward advancing our scientific insight into human social behavior. To have the courage to explore a new paradigm one may be tempted to believe that one's intellectual ancestry must be rejected or, at least, ignored. That if one wants to assert something really new, a degree of rejection and ignorance of the past is helpful and even somewhat necessary. Yet one can overdo such bravado. There comes a time when some attention to a paradigm's ancestry may be helpful. It can serve to clarify the new paradigm.

What sort of science underlies this book's offering? What is its heritage from the social sciences? What is its intellectual pedigree? Where, in the recent past, does it have roots?

Its roots are in the school of Symbolic Interaction that had its fruition in the sociology department of the University of Chicago in the 1940s. The present volume owes much to this school. Yet it also constitutes a rather drastic rejection of some of that school's perspective to science.

In a sense, this book is a third generation of symbolic interaction study of human behavior. The first, the formative period was under such University of Chicago scholars as Everett Hughes, who followed in the footsteps of an earlier generation of scholars, notably William I. Thomas, Charles Cooley, Robert Park, Georg Simmel and George H. Mead. From their work emerged a blending of social anthropology––with its emphasis on field work and personal involvement of the researcher in one's scientific work––with sociology and interactionist psychology. This created the view that the scientist, personally, was a primary instrument for discovering the social nature of human beings. That scientist would be trained through a kind of apprenticeship under a master teacher-scholar-researcher. From it one would "get the feel," the sensitivity, for both immersing oneself into and, also, understanding the immediacy of situations of social life. The method of participant-observation was born.

From it emerged a second generation of scholars, all trained at Chicago, who practiced this artful science after they moved on to other settings. Perhaps the most brilliant craftsman to come out of the Chicago school was Erving Goffman, who produced books that quickly became classics of the symbolic interaction genre––notably *The Presentation of Self in Everyday Life* and *Asylums*. In the 1990s, the name of Morris Schwartz came to popular attention via a book titled *Tuesdays with Morrie*, which vividly described this Chicago alumnus's profound impact on his students at Brandeis University, demonstrating how to "live" one's artful science while dying. The ways of living one's artful science was incorporated most fully in a number of university based programs in medical sociology that emerged from the Chicago school.

The Chicago School recently had a masterful resurgence in Alice Goffman's book 'On the Run'. Perhaps not surprisingly, Alice Goffman is the daughter of Erving Goffman.

My teacher, Harvey Smith, was also a prominent alumnus of the Chicago school. He established a program of medical sociology at the University of North Carolina at Chapel Hill. There I encountered him and his considerable artistry in the teaching and practice of symbolic interaction. Although sociology at the University of North Carolina was by then a heartland of statistical empirical social science, it still had sufficient residue of humanistic science from the Howard Odum-Rupert Vance era to permit entry of the Northern, urbane symbolic interaction phenomenon.

In the person of Harvey Smith—presiding over a small academic empire in medical sociology—there flourished a close focus on personal engagement in the practice of participant observation sociology. Smith's wondrous verbal skills were on constant display for the training of students in the craft of "doing" sociology through personal immersion in a situation of social interaction and talking about it. Talking. Always talking. For Smith, such verbal sociology was a way of life. It burst forth in an atmosphere of intellectual ebullience that affected everyone within earshot. There was considerable excitement. Its target was immediacy, seen as a life force comprised of direct, person-to-person interactions. Smith and many of the other symbolic interactionists would illuminate these interactions with incredible insights, producing a particularly vibrant social psychology.

Yet Smith—as did many other symbolic interactionists—gave short shrift to some facets of science. Tough-minded replicability of one's findings was not in his vocabulary. Nor was the search for order taken seriously. Instead, he was vitally interested in process, in flux, in savoring events as they occurred in the daily interactions of flesh and blood persons. Structure—the framing of person-to-person interactions, the catalysts and anchorages behind them— had little place in this intellectual universe.

This was the beginning of my discomfort with symbolic interaction sociology, which, to put it plainly, was then paying my way through graduate school with a fellowship under Harvey Smith's medical sociology program. As I indicate in the Dedication of this book, I had imbibed a good deal of the science intoxication of Alfred North Whitehead in my undergraduate days. From it I came to realize that the artistry of symbolic interaction omitted some of the cornerstones of serious science. To this realm the present book tries to contribute.

I am equally disenchanted with what currently goes for serious science in sociology. Namely, only worth studying is what can be counted, measured and is statistically quantifiable. These certainly can get at useful and important aspects of what goes on in nature. But much more fundamental to science is the search for orderliness behind what is countable and measurable and, indeed, readily visible in nature. When physicists point to constructs such as Gravitation and Relativity, and chemists point to the Periodic Table, they are identifying particular forms of orderliness in nature which, to put it differently, form frames behind the flux we see and hear around us. To be sure, the identified "orderliness" can sometimes be tested and refined by quantification. But quantification is merely the icing on top of the cake. Far more basic is what is underneath: the particular forms of orderliness.

This book's focus on immediacy has its roots in symbolic interaction. But it tries to supply a sense of vital orderliness––of structure––that can underlie human social behavior and thereby augments the focus on flux and ephemeral acts of much traditional work in symbolic interaction. I have tried to show how the five constructs chosen for this book's attention can serve as such underlyings for human social behavior. They may, in themselves, become catalysts, anchorage points, and even vehicles for producing specific phenomena, such as those described under the discussion of "The Second Path" (as vehicles of transformation in the life of individuals), "The World of Riders" (as vehicles of impingings of one situation into another), and "The Case of Bounded Indeterminacy" (as vehicles of the operation of unknowables that can sustain systems).

From these findings the new paradigm is urging itself on us by pointing to a new class of phenomena that need attention. It leads to new insights and new explanations and, at the same time, it opens up new unanswered questions. The work is surely unfinished. This must not deter us from taking the steps to explore and taste the riches of the new paradigm. I invite you to join in this venture.

Transcendence of Immediacy: Introduction

The immediacy of one's daily life sometimes contains such strain, such unbearable pain, such convulsion, that only a transcendence of one's immediate situation can enable life to continue. This can happen when we encounter extreme physical pain, extreme emotional suffering––as in the sudden and unexpected loss of a loved one––and extreme moral dislocation aroused when all one has believed and valued seems to have evaporated.

At such times we look to ways of transcending our immediate situation. When we find it, we may be able to continue to live our lives, because we have restructured that immediate situation. Here transcendence enables us to adapt to our immediate situation.

The actual mechanisms we use to achieve transcendence vary greatly. They may range from psychological withdrawal from the situation in which we find ourselves––denying that there is any need to respond at all––to its polar opposite of bringing into our situation entirely new, "other-worldly" elements, such as embracing a religious cult's promise of immediate salvation. In the following essays I shall touch on these and other mechanisms.

The essay based on Viktor Frankl's encounter with a dying woman at the Auschwitz concentration camp illustrates personal transcendence of extreme horror in one's immediate circumstances. On the verge of death, the woman discovers what is perhaps life's deepest secret and greatest prize––the capacity to recognize and somehow capture ultimate meaning

1

in one's life. Her beatitude is achieved by finding a way to transcend the immediacy of her current suffering. In gratitude she ends up thanking her Auschwitz fate.

The essays on prayer and cults emphasize that finding a bridge to transcendence, be it through prayer or the offerings of a cult, caters to a fundamental human need. That need to transcend one's immediate situation is most clear and pressing during great personal pain, as in times of sudden bereavement. Yet even when the need is not currently with us, we may try to keep our bridges to transcendence intact through prayer to a transcending God, whose powers can be called on in times of crisis and trauma. Prayer is frequently couched in terms of praising the transcendence of a divine being. Of course God does not need to be reminded about having transcendent powers. Actually our prayers are geared to maintain some access to transcendence in our own life. We want, and sometimes desperately feel the need for, access to a transcendent God because we need to transcend our current situation.

The essay on Hitler as a false messiah discusses how transcendence can be offered to an entire nation. Hitler succeeded in transforming much of Germany's social order into an instrument for reaching transcendence, namely pursuing an illusionary, otherworldly dream of German national grandeur. In the final analysis, Hitler ended up trampling on some of the very values he had proclaimed. On a smaller scale, the essay on cults also touches on the manipulation of an entire community. Cults, too, promise to bring transcendence into the life of their members.

The essay on personal moral virility begins with realizing that an individual's sense of identity is frequently based on believing that one is somehow linked to a larger, a transcendent, moral order. But one's sense of being alive, of personal virility, is based on more than an abstract belief in such a moral order. Most importantly, it is based on one's conviction that one deserves that linkage because one is making an active contribution to that moral order. We hear it expressed in such statements as "I am an American; I vote and pay my taxes," and "I am a family man; I don't chase after women." Here transcendence is grasped through one's personal contribution to a moral order. Its most extreme version is demonstrated by religious cult members. They sometimes contribute their property, their energy, their sexuality, and their lives with a sense of moral rectitude and joy.

On a lesser scale, our daily sense of having worth is continually nurtured by our belief that we are actively contributing to a value larger than ourselves. This does not have to be focused on any grandiose sense of contributing to human betterment. Even the pursuit of making money is, for many Americans, deemed to be a large and morally worthy value to which one ought to contribute precisely because it links one to a value larger than oneself. This, like one's link to the service of others, can contribute meaning to one's life. The essence here is not the particular content of one's values. The essence is one's sense of being connected to a worthy value that goes beyond oneself, and making the connection come alive by one's active contribution to that value. By being an active contributor to that larger value, one derives a sense of moral virility. One is a full-fledged member of that value's domain. Under it one stands upright.

Transcending One's Immediate World: *Revisiting Viktor Frankl*

Viktor Frankl's book *Man's Search for Meaning: An Introduction to Logotherapy* (1) is surely one of the most remarkable books to emerge from the Holocaust. This is the work of a professional psychiatrist who personally experienced the horrors of Auschwitz. This is the work of an individual who managed to survive these horrors through a combination of moral courage and intellectual vision; an individual who later committed himself to sharing what he discovered, not only by caring for his patients, but also by participating in the intellectual world of research, teaching and publication. That intellectual world is inherently open-ended and, to the extent that it is alive and vibrant, it is always unfinished. I want to honor Frankl by building within that region of the open-ended world to which he so valiantly pointed us.

Frankl supplies us with the story of a young woman, an Auschwitz inmate, who knew she was going to die very soon, but who discovered in her suffering a sublime meaning in her life. Frankl in his role as physician talks to the dying woman. She is lying on a bunk, facing a window through which part of a tree is visible. She is no longer able to move. She tells him that she has found great spiritual contentment here, in her suffering at Auschwitz––far more than she had ever experienced in her previous, rather affluent life. "I am grateful that fate has hit me so hard."[2] And she valued the contribution of her "only friend... in my loneliness."[3] That friend was the tree, visible through the window. She reports that she talks to the tree. Frankl, thinking she might be delirious, asks whether the tree answers her. "Oh, yes," she tells him. "It says to me, I am here––I am here––I am life, eternal life."[4]

Here, surely, is a link to a larger spiritual world, which transcends the physical world––the world of pain and suffering––in which the young woman exists before her death. That spiritual world, once she accepts it, nurtures her while she exists in a world of utter desolation. That spiritual world introduces a vital partnership into her desolation: She is no longer alone. In a world of endings and death, the spiritual element provides

4

the continuity of "eternal life." The spiritual world is a rider, a link, that fundamentally transforms the meaning of her current reality. The tree is the symbol and catalyst that gives her access to that rider. It enables the rider––the link to the spiritual world––to enter into her world and transform its meaning altogether.

All this is achieved by a focused use of her existing autonomy, her use of the choices available to her. She uses them to move her mental life in a particular direction. Through these choices she reaches out to and allows herself to be embraced by an external, spiritual world. Whether the spiritual world "really" exists in an objective sense is irrelevant. What is relevant, what counts, is that to this dying woman the spiritual world is entirely and profoundly real. It is tangible; it is practical; it is immediate. For her, perhaps the most surprising development in her life is that somehow she found an access to that spiritual world. For us, the onlookers, we must acknowledge that it required an active decision, a choice to accept the tree as the messenger from a spiritual world. It enlarged her world, so that she was able to transcend, in some way at least, the horrors of Auschwitz.

At the risk of oversimplifying, Frankl's overall theme is that the heart of human existence lies in the need each human being has to find meaning in one's life. Finding meaning (in Frankl's view) is a personal journey. Every one of us must find it by and for oneself. Furthermore, meaning can be found through three avenues:

(1) by deeds or work, such as being creative in one's career or through specific activities, be they artistic, scientific, or humanistic;

(2) by love and appreciation––of some aspects of nature, or of a person (or both); and,

(3) "by the attitude we take to unavoidable suffering."(5) (Concerning "unavoidable" suffering: If the suffering is avoidable it should, ordinarily, be avoided. Avoidable suffering is not, in Frankl's sense, an appropriate source of enlightened meaning.) The individual can find meaning, and a reason for living, from the unavoidable suffering one experiences. One does so by transcending that suffering through the attitude taken in response to the suffering. This can lead to a very meaningful existence amid and beyond the suffering, as demonstrated by the young woman.

Here, even more than in the first two avenues, individuals actively contribute a response to what the world has handed them. The "meaning" of each individual's existence emerges from a combination of the impact of the raw environment on that individual plus the individual's response to that environment. One has some choice as to the kind of response one makes––the attitude one adopts toward the environment, how one interprets what is happening.

An important insight Frankl provides is that the individual who discovers meaning in unavoidable suffering does so because of the human capacity to transcend the situation in which one exists. Frankl shows us that this capacity can have a profound impact: It can make the difference between living and dying. Within these extremes, it can determine the quality of life we lead. For example, in some camps there was the *Musselman*––the individual who had given up on life, who had totally renounced any connectedness to one's life beyond the camp, and who was the antithesis of the young woman Frankl described. For the *Musselman* life had no meaning; one would surely die soon (even if one were in fairly good physical health), but, unlike the young woman, one's death was a death of utter desolation since one had already died before death.

Yet in Frankl's work, the actual *process* of transcendence––its component parts and mechanisms––remains rather vague and elusive. One can easily fall into the trap of thinking that it involves mystical and extra-normal processes. I am convinced that we need not resort to mysticism or other forms of esoteric reasoning to understand and explain transcendence.

As Frankl describes it, transcendence ties in well with my research on personal autonomy, one's capacity to make choices within the context of social situations[6]––and on riders, the overarching imprint from an external source, that can color all component parts of a particular social situation.[7]

Concerning autonomy: My starting point is that every individual has some autonomy––some capacity to make choices, no matter what circumstances or social pressures impinge on that individual. The dying woman described by Frankl had choices. So did the *Musselman*. In each case, the choices revolve around how one responds mentally to the world in which one currently exists.

First, the claim that every individual has some autonomy: Surely a prisoner in jail has no autonomy, no freedom to make choices, which seems to defy what I just said. After all, the prisoner is forced to spend one's time in a particular place, is told with whom one can and cannot associate, where and when to sleep, what to eat, and so on. The controls that curtail the prisoner's life seem all-pervasive. Yet listing the controls over the prisoner's life misses a crucial zone in which the prisoner has a great deal of autonomy: the freedom to be active, even to be inventive and creative.

The prisoner has the autonomy to hate the confining authorities and to nurture that hatred, sometimes in elaborately creative ways. Indeed, the very controls over the prisoner's life by the prison administration—the manifold assaults on his or her dignity—help establish mental zones within which the prisoner's resentment is fostered and nurtured. The prison authorities virtually plead with the prisoner: "Please hate us." Each act of punitive control by authorities is an invitation for some form of active hatred in return. Here the prisoner has autonomy to exercise creativity in the form of active and focused nurturing of hatred for the confining authorities.

When trying to understand how people behave in a particular situation, the question that needs to be answered is not whether they have any autonomy—any freedom of action, any capacity to make choices—but the kinds of autonomy they have in that particular situation in which they currently live. What are the zones of behavior in which they have autonomy—such as a prisoner's autonomy to hate the prison staff, and the use of that autonomy to create and maintain a culture of hatred toward that staff.

Concerning riders: I shall argue that in the case of the dying Auschwitz patient, the "meaning" she discovered and which permeates her remaining life is due to a *rider process*—a particular piece of external reality that makes an imprint on her current state. To illustrate this process, here is another, very different example of a rider, showing the process of imprinting by an external reality.

In the early years of the Vietnam War, the "body count" was a prominent and much publicized feature. Progress of the war was reported in terms of how many enemy soldiers had been killed in the latest battle. In practice, this meant that U.S. troops, especially the officers, were judged by their superiors on the criterion of how many enemy soldiers their own men had killed. Its source was the American military machine finding a way to demonstrate in tangible form––to the politicians and to the public–– that the war effort was successful. The body count became a rider that permeated much of the ongoing actions by individual American soldiers." It often influenced what they did on the battlefield and how they judged their own actions. This included making up exaggerated body counts as well as occasional willingness to kill civilians (as at the My Lai massacre) in order to raise the body count. One's military actions "made sense" by their bearing on the body count. It was the master rider that defined how soldiers were expected to assess their participation in the war.

Riders depict a larger reality that colors all aspects of a particular situation. They constitute a link of specific actions to an external and wider context. In the case of the body count in Vietnam, the link is to the U.S. government and the broader American society's sense of urgency (during the early years of the war) about having the conflict come to a victorious conclusion. The government, through the Department of Defense and the military staff, brought this urgency to bear on the local field commanders. Concretely, this was spelled out in the demand from the soldier in the field: "What are you doing to help win the war? Are you contributing to the body count?" In short, the body count rider was very tangible in the way it linked the local situation to a wider reality during the early years of the Vietnam War.

By contrast, during the later years of the war, a new, larger reality came to dominate the war––and became a rider to the life of the participants, including long personal emotional turmoil for many of them after they came back to the United States. That new reality questioned the legitimacy of the war, on moral grounds, on political grounds and even on practical military grounds. Coping with that rider became a long-standing personal issue for many Vietnam veterans. It sometimes took the form of the query, "What did you do to *end* the war?", as against the earlier query, "What are you doing to *win* the war?"

A particular item, such as the body count, becomes the symbol that links a specific local situation to another wider reality, just as the tree became the symbol that linked the Auschwitz woman to a wider reality.

Establishing the link requires that the individual participant in the local situation accepts, in one's own autonomous way, that this linkage is indeed real and justified. When accepted, the link becomes very powerful because it produces a larger meaning to one's situation. It permits entry into the local situation of the wider linked world, which the individual, through the use of one's autonomy, then translates into action. In the case of the Vietnam War, acceptance of the body count rider meant accepting the pressures and "reality" as defined by the military authorities. This justified killing the enemy. It became one's mandate, one's duty. One then used autonomy––choices, initiative, focused energy––to implement that duty.

The case of the Auschwitz inmate who discovers meaning in her suffering, as Frankl describes it, also requires use of autonomy, namely, using it to establish a linkage to a larger spiritual world. This, in turn, requires switching on a particular zone of autonomy––and switching off other zones, notably, stopping to concentrate one's imagination and feelings on pain and suffering. Instead, one turns–– in one's imagination––to another world. In Frankl's own case, for example, at a time when he had almost unbearable pain in his foot, he turned his thoughts to giving a scholarly lecture to an academic audience, as he had done before he came to Auschwitz and as he hoped to do again afterward. That world suddenly became so real and powerful that it wiped out the suffering and pain he was currently experiencing. It imported new meaning into his situation.

Specific symbols, such as remembering his wife's love and his satisfying professional career, served as catalysts for activating a rider of an external life that came to pervade Frankl's ongoing life at Auschwitz. This process sustained him in a very tangible way. It wiped out the pain in his foot. On a broader level, it enabled him to cope with many of the physical and emotional assaults on his person.

Frankl was thereby exercising "external" autonomy, namely living and participating in a world that was outside the one in which he currently lived physically. He was, at the same time, renouncing internal autonomy, namely not attending to some features of the world in which he actually existed at that time, specifically, the pain in his foot.

I am well aware of the opposite extreme, of the phenomenon of the *Musselman* in some concentration camps, as mentioned previously. These are persons who had totally given up on life, on participating (even in

9

imaginary ways) in the external world they had once known, and who were therefore inevitably going to die very soon. They had abandoned external autonomy altogether and, as a result, their lives were going to end very soon. Perhaps they had so exclusively concentrated on internal autonomy, dwelling on their current pain and suffering, that it extinguished their external autonomy altogether. Concretely, then, as the pain became unbearable it left only one kind of autonomy, the active abandonment of life. This too included an exercise of autonomy in the form of one final decision: to abandon one's life to whatever assaults came. If there was a rider to their current life, it may be called an embracing affirmation of death. It was all-pervasive, affecting every act. To an outside observer, it seemed that mental rigor mortis had set in even before physical death had taken place. But to the *Musselman*, this might not be true. One might have a richly focused inner life in the remaining days of one's existence. Perhaps it centered on celebrating one's death—"living it" to the fullest.

Frankl points out that the search for meaning is inevitably personal and private. Each individual travels a personal road, and one has to construct one's own road while traveling on it. But in human history there have been enough private and personal spiritual journeys so that their residues—such as those found in the form of organized and recorded religious doctrines— provides a reservoir from which we can draw as we go about constructing a life journey. For many persons formal religion provides the linkage to a spiritual world that supplies meaning to one's life. There, the conception of a supreme being or participation in religious ritual (or both) can be the lanterns that guide one's personal autonomy, and keep that autonomy from dissipating in frantic private searches for meaning to one's life.

Yet at times, as the young woman of Auschwitz demonstrates, it is not a specific religion that comes to the rescue but the explicit and focused use of one's autonomy to reach out to a wider spiritual world and then to establish a viable link to it.

The intellectual issue—indeed the scientific issue—is that what Frankl calls transcendence of one's immediate situation (as, for example, when an Auschwitz inmate transcends the horrors of Auschwitz) is actually the human capacity to establish linkage among situations that, physically and temporally, are widely separate.

In the evolution of human beings, this capacity to establish linkage among physically and temporally separate events has surely become a fundamental characteristic of our ongoing social existence, now highlighted by the Internet and communications revolution. We lead our lives by actively including features that transcend the immediate situation in which we find ourselves. We can do so because of our capacity to use symbols. Not only do symbols enable us to make connections, and disconnections, but they also can be the catalysts that enable distant events to intrude into our immediate world as riders. These riders can define our current situation; they can permeate our perspective and our actions and give a sense of meaning to them.

The bearing of symbols and riders is certainly not something unique to the horrors of Auschwitz. Symbols and riders bear on our lives much of the time. We are silently attuned to them as we go about our daily activities. In this chapter I merely want us to become aware of how they bear on the search for meaning in one's life under painful circumstances.

Frankl taught us that we can find meaning for our lives, no matter how miserable and depraved our condition. We can do so because we can expand our personal world by transcending the painful tyranny of the immediate situation in which we find ourselves. As we transcend that immediacy, we can link ourselves to a more benign external reality.

In short, the process by which we can find meaning goes beyond being introspective, of searching within––be it within ourselves or within the immediate context in which we find ourselves. To the contrary, it centers on the outside, on transcendence, and then establishing a linkage to that more benign outside reality. Let us therefore amend Rene Descartes'––"I think, therefore I am"––by recognizing that <u>I can transcend, therefore my life can have meaning.</u>

NOTES

1 Viktor E. Frankl, *Man's Search for Meaning: An Introduction to Logotherapy*, 3rd ed. (New York: Simon and Schuster, Touchstone Books, 1984).

2 Ibid., p. 78.

3 2 Ibid.

4 Ibid.

5 Ibid., 115.

6 Fred Emil Katz, *Autonomy and Organization: The Limits of Social Control* (New York: Random House, 1968); Fred Emil Katz, *Structuralism in Sociology* (Albany, NY: State University of New York Press, 1976), chap. 3.

7 Fred Emil Katz, *Ordinary People and Extraordinary Evil: A Report on the Beguilings of Evil* (Albany, NY: SUNY Press, 1993), esp. pp. 37-40. For further discussion of riders, see later parts of the present book.

8 Ibid., pp. 104-105.

Bridges to Transcendence:
Why We Praise God While Coping with Extreme Sickness, Death, and Misfortune

While taking part in Jewish religious services I have often wondered why we devote so much effort to praising God. Christians and Muslims doubtlessly also devote much effort to the praise of God––Muslims' declaration that Allah is Great immediately comes to mind, as do the Christian adorations of Jesus Christ. But I am particularly aware of it in the prayers of my fellow Jews. On a typical Sabbath, our prayers practically gush in praise of God. It seems that we cannot find enough exemplary things to say about God, not enough adjectives to describe the praiseworthiness, glories and grandeur of God. Even the basic prayer of mourning, the *Kaddish*, begins with "Magnified and sanctified be the name of God" and includes "Exalted and honored be the name of the Holy One."

Does God really need our singing His (or Her) praise? Does God need our exaltations about the grandeur and majesty of His (or Her) attributes? Are we simply trying to bribe God by making Him feel good so that He will do nice things for us? Surely not. Does God need validation from us? Surely not. Does God need us to cheer Him on to keep doing the good things He has done in the past? Surely not. What is going on when we exuberantly sing the praise of God? Why do we do so?

These issues came to a head for me during a service that addressed the issue of how our prayers––and our religiosity altogether––cope with extreme illness, suffering, death and other personal crises. What does my faith have to offer––what does any religion have to offer––in these situations? How, if at all, does it help us cope with pain, with heartfelt indignation about unjustified suffering, with shattered dreams and destroyed meanings of life?

In these circumstances, what is the role of prayer? Some argue that it is indeed helpful in lessening suffering, even in promoting healing for those who are terribly ill. But, they claim, this does not necessarily require a religious content. One can pray to a humanistic commonality of humankind, where "God" is not a factor; one can have support groups of well-disposed individuals jointly focusing on the suffering of the individual and, thereby, creating a human bond that will lessen suffering and pain.

It seems to me that the underlying issue in these efforts is the same one that underlies religious prayer: There is an effort to create transcendence of the seeming hopelessness of the moment by moving into a zone where hope still exists; transcendence of one's present pain and suffering by envisioning a state where pain and suffering are no longer all-pervasive; transcendence of the current meaninglessness of life to a condition where meaning returns. Doubtless, secular group activities and nonreligious "prayers" may indeed achieve such transcendence. But so may religious prayer.

Here we must return to the glorification of God. It seems to me that what we are doing when we glorify God, when we sing God's praise, is trying to nurture our own transcendence. As we praise and proclaim the glory of a transcending God, we are actually working to build, and keep in good repair, bridges for our own transcendence. God's transcendence is not the final issue. Our own transcendence is the final issue. It is our yearned-for objective. It is our weaponry against overwhelming misfortune and pain.

We can achieve our own transcendence through access to a transcending God. That access constitutes our proximity to transcendence. Through it alone we see our way to transcending the ongoing vicissitudes in life.

We draw on our access to God's transcendence in times of extreme trouble and pain. Before such occasions of extreme need arise we try to have transcendence available by keeping our access to it in good repair. Furthermore, we want to make sure it is within our reservoir, our storehouse, available for use when we need it. We don't simply want to be able to draw on it when we ourselves need it. We also, at times, try to share it with loved ones when they, in turn, are having to cope with overwhelming issues. Transcendence is infectious. It is sharable without being diminished. It is not a zero sum.

Here, then, is a religious route, a transcendent God-centered route, to personal transcendence. It can be a distinctive and vital resource for coping with extreme tribulations that come into the individual's life.

It is quite possible that the secular techniques for transcendence are valuable and valid for those who choose them. Yet the religious center—the

God-centered one—is also valuable and valid. For most of us who, in some measure at least, are religious, the bridge to transcendence exists through our access to a transcending God. We frequently remind ourselves of God's transcendence through our prayers. We try to keep our own connection to it in good repair through ritual observances, in addition to our prayers that acknowledge God's transcendent existence. The access to transcendence is vital to our spiritual well-being, most especially during misfortune and sickness that tests our faith in everything we have come to believe and expect in life.

In a sense, when it comes to transcendence, we are in partnership with God. What God's actual attributes are, we cannot know. But what we do know is that we can attribute transcendent attributes to God. We can attempt to have access to the God having such attributes. We can then come to have a measure of proximity and access to such transcendence, which will help us cope with issues in our own life. In all of this, we are God's partners precisely through acknowledging God's vastly superior transcendence.[1]

Finally, a word about how total transcendence might actually be experienced, how it feels. Perhaps it is a sublime sense of freedom. Here is a report by a passenger in a plane at the moment its pilot abruptly took extreme evasive action to prevent collision with another plane. The passenger, not knowing why the plane suddenly appeared to break apart, was fully convinced that he was about to die. He states: "My life, past, present and future, was suddenly hysterically irrelevant, and in the kind of eternity that can reside inside a second, my past and future, my memories, my whole life was insanely and laughably absurb . . . . within the wonder, beauty, irony and absurdity of that momentary eternity was a kind of freedom I had never known. In facing the nothingness of death, I saw the irrelevance of the desires and goals and regrets that had defined my life—and I got free of them, free of everything, absolutely free."[2] Here, it seems, is an experience of feeling total transcendence.

NOTES

1 Freud cites his friend Roman Rolain as saying that the core of religiosity is "a feeling which he would like to call a sensation of 'eternity'—a feeling of something limitless, unbounded . . . it is a source of religious energy." (Sigmund Freud, *Civilization and its Discontents* [New York: W. W. Norton, 1961], p. 11.) This "feeling" comes very close to what I am calling the sense of transcendence. However, I must add that Freud immediately attacked his friend's idea.

2 Robert Burrus, "The divine irony of the last laugh," *The Sun* (Baltimore), May 14, 1997, p. 11 A.

Cults:
Once Again We Are Surprised and Shocked

In 1997, in the vicinity of San Diego, thirty-nine members of the Heaven's Gate cult committed suicide.

Why? How could this have happened? Each time we hear of such an event, such as the mass deaths at Jonestown, in Guyana, we are surprised and shocked. Cult members seem to depart widely from what we regard as normal human behavior. This is why we are so surprised and stunned. Perhaps we have a vested interest, in order to preserve our own sanity, in describing cultists who commit suicide as crazy, as deviants who are utterly different from the rest of us. It is time that we examine some of our own thinking about the nature of cults. It turns out that we have created a mythology of our own that continues to deceive us—and causes us to be shocked—whenever cults confront us with such monstrous acts as mass suicides.

The Heaven's Gate mass suicide teaches us something precisely because it breaks with our popular mythology about such behavior. Two pieces of that mythology stand out. First, we assume that participants in such mass suicides must be totally isolated from the rest of us in order to engage in such behavior; they must be physically separate, so as not to have any contact with the relatively sane, everyday world in which most of us live. Yet in San Diego the cultists had "outside" jobs; they were free to come and go from the domicile where they lived. They had contact with the outside world. They interacted with people in the local community. Through the Internet, they were in contact with a vast number of people beyond their immediate San Diego neighbors. Psychologically, the Heaven's Gate cultists may have lived in a separate world, but they were not physically isolated, at least not totally.

Second, we assume that cultists who kill themselves in unison must, surely, be under the total control of a leader. They must be zombies who no longer have any autonomy whatsoever. They surely simply carry out the bidding of a crazed, and usually unscrupulous, guru who is their leader. We blame it all on that leader. A headline in the *Washington Post* (March 30,

1997) reads: "Surrender of Self Is the Key to Cult Life." The followers are no longer functioning human beings. They have totally given themselves over to a leader.

Yet, by all evidence, the Heaven's Gate cultists did not act like zombies, devoid of any will of their own. They performed fairly complicated work assignments on the outside, for which they got paid and for which they earned respect. They carried themselves with dignity and even continued to uphold such standard American orthodoxies as a love of fine cars and clothes. And, former members tell us, within their communal living there was much laughter, discussion, joyful living. Popular analyses stubbornly ignore these facts while insisting on the doleful description of cult life as blindly obedient to a crazed leader and devoid of personal independence, dignity, and joy.

In our zeal to picture the cultists as crazy, we concentrate on the message they were following. The Heaven's Gate cultists fully expected to be picked up by a space ship and transported to another universe. Extraterrestrial beings are going to come here and bring them to that other domain. If these do not show up, then another form of conveyance to the other domain must be found––such as leaving one's earthly body. But putting ourselves in the place of people without our own upbringing, is it really so very different from our own beliefs in a "soul," in a "heaven" to which we may go after our death here, on this earth? We are comfortable with our own beliefs, with our particular brand of mysticism and unverifiable components, but are uncomfortable with other people's beliefs and their "strange" content.

Of course the cultists' belief in their pending space travel to another domain is empirically groundless and impossible to verify. It is pure mysticism––as are some of our own beliefs and articles of faith.

But all this is quite beside the point. The real issue is not what people actually believe. It is not a matter of one belief being more valid than another; it is not a matter of whether one belief is right and the other belief is wrong; or whether one belief is inherently crazy and the other belief is inherently sane. The real issue is the human yearning for transcendence–– for overcoming life's turbulence and uncertainties, for coming to terms with the death and suffering of loved ones, for the discovery of meaning for one's existence amid the trivia and pettiness of daily living. This lies at the heart of much appeal of formal religions. They show the way beyond the immediacies in which we find ourselves––the pain, sorrow, disappointment, and frustration––and the uncertainties about what lies beyond us, beyond ourselves, beyond the present circumstances that are, at times, so trying and hurtful, so challenging to any faith and confidence in ourselves.

What applies to formal religions applies even more to cults and other mystical programs. They, too, claim to give answers to the most troubling questions that confront us. But they do so by inviting the member to participate in what seems to be a most wondrously effective and personal way.

Cults (and religions) do far more than just offer "answers" to troubling questions. Their most profound impact does not come from their "answers," the content of their beliefs, the particular predictions and formulations about the nature of reality. By any rational assessment the formulations, the theories about reality, of many cults are simply quite silly. But this does not matter. Not to the believer, not to the cultist.

What does matter is how members are participating in transcendence–– and thereby believe they achieve the highest form of self-realization to which they could possibly aspire. Whether you call it access to salvation, union with a larger universal entity, or achieving sublime ecstasy, the individual feels that transcendent bliss is at hand through one's participation and contribution. It is at hand, here and now. It is present and palpable–– through one's own participation.

Participation is crucial. One's transcendence––one's salvation, whatever the cult calls it––is not simply handed to you. You *earn* it by your participation in the cult's program, by your contributions, by giving of yourself, your property, your diligence, your energy. What greater gift can you possibly give than your life? Donating your life, in the form of suicide, can be seen, and is seen by many cultists, as the highest gift in the service of the highest and noblest form of transcendent fusion with an ultimate reality.

The final mysticism we outsiders stick to is that no one could possibly do such things as mass suicide of their own free will. The cultists must be operating under extreme duress––be it physical duress or total brainwashed mental duress. To this I answer that this is a misperception. The cultists feel exceedingly free. They do, in fact, have a great deal of personal autonomy even while going to their death in suicidal passion.

Our confusion springs from the notion that such people could not possibly have any autonomy, any freedom of choice, any capacity to make decisions on their own. This is a profound misreading of how human autonomy actually works when we find ourselves in social contexts. I have been studying autonomy for over thirty years.[1] I am convinced that people can have autonomy in the unlikeliest situations. Usually, the real issue is not whether people have autonomy, but what sort of autonomy they do have. In the case of the cults, we see distinctive zones in which people have autonomy and exercise it to the fullest. They have considerable autonomy to demonstrate their commitment to the sublime cause that the guru has set before them. He or she is the catalyst, setting out the social format of where and how autonomy exists. But it is the member, the participating cultist who then fills in the blanks by donating one's contributions—such as energy and enthusiasm, work, occupational skills, property, sexuality, and, finally, one's life. The cultist sees all these as voluntary contributions, freely donated to the grand cause.

For the cultist, there is a sense of unmatched fulfillment and joy in the act of contributing to ultimate transcendence. That ultimate transcendence—that reaching of one's highest yearnings—is about to take place here and now. One's own freely given contribution is crucial to making it happen. What greater glory could there possibly be?

If we refuse to see the power of this seductive process, we will be forever surprised and shocked by cults. Each new cult will again startle us, even as it exacts it terrible price.

Suicide as a weapon

In the discussion about cults I have not taken up the current wave of suicide deliberately used as a weapon of terrorist warfare. This phenomenon creates a new twist to the nature and uses of suicide.

Among cultists suicide is apparently carried out joyfully, in the expectation that one is now achieving final bliss. One is enraptured by the conviction that one is reaching ultimate fulfillment, ultimate glory by embracing a world beyond ours, beyond the here and now. It is as transcendent venture.

In the terrorism scenario, suicide is apparently also carried out joyfully. But it is under the conviction that one is using the bluntest weapon – one's very life – to achieve a profoundly this-worldly objective. It targets a specifically identified population that is deemed to be beyond redemption – people representing the ultimate, godless, dangerously contaminating evil. One's suicide will remove that ultimate contamination from the here and now. It is an act of purification. In its own way it, too, is seen as a transcendent venture.

Fred Emil Katz

NOTES

1   See Fred Emil Katz, *Autonomy and Organization: The Limits of Social Control* (New York: Random House, 1968); Fred Emil Katz, *Structuralism in Sociology: An Approach to Knowledge* (Albany, NY: SUNY Press, 1976).

The Case of the False Messiah:
Adolf Hitler

The Ultimate becomes Immediate. Once this idea is embraced, it impassions people. It opens up entire zones of action into which people fling themselves with utmost fervor, believing that transcendence is in their grasp.

The advent of Adolf Hitler in Germany is remarkable in many ways. He was an Austrian by birth, not a German, who became Germany's leader. Here was man who harnessed the German people's fears and aspirations in ways that made them willing to engage in deeds beyond comprehension, make sacrifices beyond compare, and adopt levels of self-deception that cross the outer boundary of sanity, entering fully into the realm of the delusional.

Among the German citizens, Hitler energized the disadvantaged, the destitute and the disenchanted. He also electrified many of the comfortably well-off, the entrenched members of the country's privileged classes. In all this he succeeded in polluting the thinking of people among whom were some of the most sophisticated and most educated people in the modern world. They joined Hitler in attempting to actualize a cosmic dream. They became his followers.

Hitler was regarded by most of these followers as a man of superhuman attributes, a man who would catapult Germany to its greatest destiny through his personal leadership. That leadership would restore, revitalize, and activate Germany's dormant energy. It would bring forth Germany's rightful glory, before which the entire world would stand in awe. On the individual German citizen Hitler would bestow a sense of personal fulfillment and pride never before experienced. He would bring many fond wishes to fruition. He embodied and personified one's innermost yearnings. In effect, he was to many, a messiah.

Therein lay Hitler's appeal, his success and the ultimate fraud of his mission. And therein, too, lies a lesson for all of us about the nature of messiahs and the people who believe in them.

I shall discuss the nature of messiahs in a very secular way––without entering fully into the difference between, say, Jewish and Christian perspectives on the messiah. I believe that Jews and Christians are not as far apart on the messiah issue as one might think. Jews believe that the messiah, who is expected to establish ultimately the rule of God on Earth, has not yet come; yet much of human life is to be lived with such nobility and decency that the messiah is likely to come. For many Jews, it is the pursuit of the coming of the messiah––of being worthy of the messiah's coming–– that constitutes a reason for living a good and worthy life. Christians, on the other hand, believe that the messiah, in the person of Jesus, has in fact already come; that, through the example of his own life, Jesus points the way to the essence of the good and worthy life; this lesson is to be implemented in the religiously grounded life, one that is worthy of the example already set. Christian belief further holds that a second coming of Christ is to happen to carry out much the same purpose envisioned by Jewish belief. In a way, both religions are messianically urging their members to pursue a worthy and good life––with a messiah as a fundamentally personal moral guide, one through whom the ordinary mortal human being can find a personalized way to transcend the mundane and enter into a tangible, realizable moral compact with a transcending moral universe. Personal salvation is facilitated through a messiah, be he postulated to come at some time in the future (in the Jewish view) or having already made an appearance on Earth (in the Christian view).

The "personal" side of the Judeo-Christian messiah vision is threefold. First, the messiah is a person who, through his or her own life, personifies the moral message. (The messiah differs from a prophet, who has a profound moral message, but whose personal life does not necessarily personify and exemplify the moral message, nor does that personal life serve as a personal vehicle for redemptive effect in people's lives as well as salvation, particularly in the Christian sense.) Second, the messiah's message is directed to the individual person––the citizen, the member of the community, the ordinary human being––in a very personal way, offering him or her a personal access to moral salvation, a personal attachment to sublime and ultimate moral grace. Third, the individual, in response to the message from the messiah, acts in moral matters in one's own life in a manner that connects to the messiah's demonstrated vision of the state of ultimate grace. Through one's actions one thereby helps to actualize the messiah's wondrous vision. In short, the individual is not passive. One actively contributes––through one's own behavior––to transforming the messiah's vision into concrete reality. One does so by actively embracing and helping to enact the messiah's vision.

I have suggested in previous writings that the difference between an actual leader and a delusional "leader" (who is apt to be found as a patient in a psychiatric facility) is that one has followers and the other does not.[1] Leaders require followers who believe in them. The followers attribute leadership qualities to the leader and legitimize leadership by their willingness to follow. Without followers, there is no leader. Those who imagine themselves to be leaders, but lack anyone to believe them probably will eventually end up in psychiatric facilities. They are defined to be living in an unreal world. The "real" world is likely to consign them to a facility in which their "unreality" is granted a limited and highly circumscribed right to exist.

In the "real" world, leadership is made up of a social compact between leader and followers. It may be explicit or implicit. But it is nonetheless a compact, an "agreement" that specifies what constraints operate on each party to the compact. It also specifies the kind and range of freedom for each party. Each has a particular zone of behavior in which it can operate rather freely, but beyond which it cannot go. And, most important, each derives distinctive benefits from the relationship.

All this is most glaringly evident when we deal with messianic leaders, individuals who exercise leadership on the basis of supposedly having extraordinary attributes. Hitler was one of these. His "extraordinary attributes" were constantly on display.

Germany had suffered a disastrous loss in World War of 1914-1918. That war had been followed by the humiliating Treaty of Versailles, in which Germany was heavily penalized. The aftermath saw economic turmoil culminating in the catastrophic rate of inflation in the 1920s. Hitler drew on all this despoiling and losses, emphasizing over and over again how unfairly Germany was being treated by her supposed enemies–– internal ones (i.e., Jews) as well as external ones. He would come to the rescue. He would return Germany to its rightful place, its glorious role in history.

Hitler was a spell-binding speaker, and he made ample use of this ability. Beginning in the 1920s, in speech after speech and in place after place, he hammered away at Germany's losses and deprivations from World War I and how he would see to it that these would be rectified. Germany's true and rightful glory would be restored. Her honor would be returned. Her economic house would be put in order. Her political power would be regained, and her military strength once more placed in a state of preeminence among the powers of the world. Her racial purity would be protected and enhanced. He personally would see to it that these things would get done; he vouched for it.

The Germans believed Hitler. The vast majority fell under his spell. Here was a man who "really understood" their secret, innermost fears and yearnings––so they thought. Here was their node of attachment to the Hitler program: They believed that he was in touch with something that concerned them profoundly. As a result, they were prepared to entrust their destiny to him. They accepted his entire package of proposed programs, those they could understand and those they could not understand; those with which they agreed and those with which they did not agree. As a result, in 1933, they elected Hitler to head the German government.

Once in office, Hitler continued his messianic style of leadership. He and his disciples proclaimed that he, above all, personified Germany's destiny. He stood between Germany and her enemies. He could see into the future. He would ennoble Germany and its people. All this was promoted and implemented in what may have been the most intensive propaganda campaign of hero worship the world has ever seen. Hitler's messiahship was deliberately and fulsomely promoted.

The propaganda machine was immensely successful. A large number of people––surely a majority of the citizenry of Germany––believed the propaganda, the speeches, and the exhortations emanating from the Nazi regime.

It is crucial that one realizes that the propaganda was not one-sided: It was not just addressed to a passive citizenry, one that simply accepted what it was told. On the contrary, the citizenry was active. They, from their side, attributed superhuman vision to Hitler. They put this into practice by believing him even when he told the most outrageous lies and followed him even when he led them into the most disastrous and lethal exploits. They attributed to Hitler supreme sensitivity to Germany's most fundamental destiny and honor. They attributed to Hitler capacities that ordinary mortals simply do not have. They did the dirty work to help bring his most deranged dreams into existence—such as participating in the murder of millions of innocent people who, supposedly, "detracted" from the "purity" of their race. Hitler, they believed, personified and made concrete the ultimate destiny of the German people. Virtually all Germans—the educated and the uneducated, the lowly under classes and the upper classes—came to believe in him as Germany's messiah.

To the individual German, Hitler's specific directives might, at times, seem drastic, harsh, and difficult to fully understand. But those directives were invariably regarded as holy writ, as emanating from the leader whose vision went beyond what ordinary mortals can see and comprehend. He was regarded as not an ordinary mortal. His messages were regarded as sacred and were treated as such.

Hitler's followers demonstrated their faith in Hitler-as-messiah not just by their intoxicated swooning and roars of approval while listening to his speeches. They translated their faith into deeds— ranging from passivity when innocent victims of Nazism were persecuted, all the way to actively participating in and contributing to such programs. It included willing participation in Hitler's military adventurisms, where their sons were very likely to be sacrificed. Hitler was granted infallibility. This, I reiterate, requires followers who actively grant this ability—who believe that the leader rightfully and actually has this ability. It is not merely a matter of a leader *claiming* to have this ability. The followers reciprocate. They grant the leader the right to act totally capriciously and arbitrarily, without having to be accountable to ordinary ways of accounting for actions. This is part of the social compact between leader and followers.

In this compact the followers retain freedom, in the form of a specific zone within which they can exercise autonomy. But that autonomy exists only in that zone, resulting in a particular kind of behavior. And it is absent from other zones. Specifically, the followers—the German citizens, in this case—have the autonomy to create ways of venerating their messiah and the cause he has personally set out for them. This ranges from donating their personal belongings, enthusiasms and energy, skills and capacities for performing work, professional expertise, up to and including donating their lives. All this is done in the service of the grand cause set before them. It is often done joyfully, with a sense that one is contributing to the most noble venture, to the ultimate destiny of one's country and person. Hitler was seen to bring ultimate reality up close, so that, by serving him, one had the unique opportunity to personally contribute to actualizing that ultimate reality. One had the once-in-a-lifetime opportunity to actually participate in the very highest form of salvation––for one's country and for one's self.

There are limits to the autonomy of followers. There are zones of behavior in which one may not exercise any autonomy at all. Most notably, one is not permitted to question the sanctity of the leader. One could not question Hitler's judgment. One could not argue against any Nazi directives that bear the imprimatur of Hitler's personal order. Perhaps the most frightening example, in all of human history, is the following.

What may be the most murderous directive of all time––the "Final Solution" to exterminate all Jews––was said to have been ordered by Hitler personally. Yet it apparently was never written down and signed, nor do we have an authenticated, witnessed and verified statement that he even gave that monstrous order verbally. The "order," so profound in its impact on the destiny of millions of human individuals, remains entirely murky. Here, surely, is the ultimate acceptance of the messianic leader's freedom from accountability. Any opposition was deemed to be a deadly sin, a vile form of moral transgression––and treated accordingly by the Nazi authorities. (The old debate over obedience to authority––that the Germans were forced to obey––entirely misses the point. Obedience to Hitler was regarded as a moral imperative, something far more powerful than the physical force behind it. Disobedience was unthinkable––and many former Nazi officials said so.)

Hitler, the messiah, also operated within constraints, within particular zones of autonomy. He had to perform miracles, and continue to do so–– hence his frantic turning to ever more daring and ever more questionable enterprises. By contrast, non-daring routines were rejected as dreary; they might have contributed to disenchantment, to demystifying the messiah. Enchantment must be nurtured. It is done through miraculous, non-routine, extraordinary deeds––such as Hitler's commanding Germany to wage war simultaneously against all the greatest powers of his era

(Great Britain, France, the Soviet Union and the United States) under the most adverse of circumstances (such as a land war against the vast Soviet Union, with its vast snow-laden regions and blizzards during winter. Hitler began that war during summer, fantasizing that he would win it before winter came; even if winter did come before the win, Germany would still prevail!). Here we have a cosmic joke: The Hitler who undertook such grotesque ventures could only do so if he actually believed his own fantasies. He no longer merely tried to deceive others. He had reached the point of deceiving himself. Here it seems, was a divine response. The grandiose deceptions had reached their final destiny, the deceiver himself.

The messiah has the autonomy to create out-of-the-ordinary happenings while, at the same time, shunning dreariness and the merely ordinary. In the latter sphere, he decidedly lacks autonomy, the capacity to participate and engage himself. The messiahs of the world must shun routines that portray their own foibles and shortcomings, of being ordinary mortal human beings. By definition, they are beyond the ordinary; this is best nurtured when they have social distance from ordinary, day-to-day human contacts. Such distance enables the followers to invent extraordinary attributes about the messiah. This is further nurtured when the life span of the messiah is short and, in particular, if the messiah dies a martyr to the cause he has espoused. Here, of course, the lives of Jesus and Martin Luther King Jr. come to mind. Both lived short lives, leaving legacies that followers are left free to amplify and elaborate. Much of the lore of messiahship is in the hands of followers—and no time more so than after the death of the messiah. Then the followers have virtually unlimited freedom to invent, or at least exaggerate, extraordinary attributes and miraculous deeds by their messiah.

In many ways, messiahs are alike. Yet, as the lives of Jesus and Martin Luther King Jr. illustrate, there surely is a world of difference between such exemplary, morally righteous individuals and the sort of messiahship demonstrated by Hitler. It is the difference between the true messiah and the false messiah. The true messiah personifies and exemplifies in his or her life the highest values of a human community. The false messiah, on the other hand, manages to attach some of the highest community values to him- or herself, but, in the final analysis, tramples on these values, destroying their viability rather than honoring them.

In the case of Hitler, this included desecrating the yearning for national community in Germany by creating a monstrous disrespect for German communal life; taking the German yearning for restoring economic and political tranquility and producing the most profound economic and political dislocation inside Germany; converting some legitimate faith in the German people's pride in their accomplishments into the most vicious forms of racism and jingoistic nationalism.

One reason why the false messiah is often very hard to expose is because followers are actively and personally involved in the messianic process. They derive a sense of personal empowerment from the messiah's message, mostly because they become heavily engaged in the process of carrying out that messianic message. They are part of the process––what I have been calling the third aspect of messiahship, namely, the individual follower's contribution to making that process work. That individual follower's contribution is very likely to include creating rationalizations, attesting to the truth of the false messiah's message, and the need to carry it forward.

Hence, when a German citizen became a functionary in the SS–– and helped design and implement the process of persecuting innocent victims of the crazed Nazi policy––he or she buttressed that participation with all sorts of personally satisfying rationalizations as to why this was really necessary. Individuals invented reasons for justifying their particular contribution. The Nazi cause became a personal cause, which, they believed, was morally justified. The followers thereby contributed much of the moral underpinnings for perpetuating the Hitler program. To be sure, theirs was a very circumscribed and limited zone of personal autonomy, it supported Hitler and refused to countenance any criticism. It underwrote the Nazi program. It helped create and nurture this false messiah. I repeat, much of the followers' personal autonomy was used to create the rationalizations–– the justifying myths––that supported the Nazi program of mass horror.

I am reminded of Dr. Eduard Wirths.[2] He was a physician who began as a very humane, caring, and courageous doctor who, in the 1930s, treated Jews secretly when this was an increasingly unpopular and risky thing for a Christian physician to do. Yet this same physician came to be a major contributor to the extermination program at Auschwitz. He devised the "selections"––deciding who would die right away and who would live a bit longer––administered by physicians when the hapless victims arrived. To justify his contribution to the campaign of horrors at Auschwitz, Dr. Wirths wrote passionate love letters to his wife. In these letters he states that he is involved in horrendous activities. But it is all worthwhile because, he feels, it will lead to a better future for their family and, in particular, for their children. With the love of his family in his heart, he can go through with the horrors.

Such is the art of rationalization––one that helped underwrite participation in horrors by an individual who started out as an unusually sensitive and courageous person. It is also a way to convert a vision of the future, here cultivated by a false messiah, into a course of action in the immediate world in which people lead their daily life. The followers believed that they are given access to their ultimate destiny––to their personal salvation––by the messiah. Given tangible access to that salvation–– surely the greatest gift one can imagine––is why many messianic leaders' followers gladly donate their lives, as well as engage in deeds that are utterly despicable from any moral point of view, even their own. Yet, there are benefits for followers. They are convinced that they attain personal access to ultimate values––a form of salvation––through this course of action.

What are the benefits for the messianic leader? What does he or she derive from the contributions of the followers? The messiah obtains validation for one's leadership. Without it, that leadership would be an empty shell, subject to rejection by the sane world. It is concrete validation of one's calling, buttressing one against the doubters and nonbelievers, augmenting one's own efforts, and providing an apparent reality test of one's purpose and mission in life. One can believe that one really is the messiah.

The lesson for all of us is that messiahs––true messiahs as well as false messiahs––can tantalizingly alert us to our innermost yearnings by providing a glimpse of ultimate moral values and do so in a form that makes these values seem attainable here and now, through our own actions. Messiahs can play with our lives––offering the grandest prize that even morally sensitive individuals can imagine––and, in the hands of the false messiah, bear the darkest Faustian cost––our souls, in the form of nurturing our willing participation in the most monstrous actions against our fellow human beings.[3]

NOTES

1   Fred Emil Katz, *Structuralism in Sociology: An Approach to Knowledge* (Albany, NY: State University of New York Press, 1976), esp. Chap. 3, "Separation and Fusion of Social Structures."

2   This is based on the study by Robert J. Lifton, *The Nazi Doctors: Medical Killing and the Psychology of Genocide* (New York: Basic Books, 1986). I discuss Dr. Wirths extensively in my book *Confronting Evil*, forthcoming.

3   I am grateful to Reverend David W. Cammack for reading this chapter and making very helpful suggestions.

Personal Moral Virility in the Immediacy of Daily Life

We humans are moral creatures. We get our sense of identity from believing that we are attached to a moral context that transcends one's own physical body. This is an orienting principle of our existence. But one's personal moral virility, one's sense of being morally alive, depends on something more: one's actions, one's contributions to that moral context and, at times, heeding dormant poisons within that context.

The moral context can take various forms. It can take the form of one's nationality––"First of all, I am an American;" "Above all, I am English;" "Deep down, I am a Spaniard." It can also take the form of one's ethnic, racial, religious, or sexual identification; or one's gang; or one's profession; or one's family. In each case, we place our primary affiliation in an entity larger than ourselves. From that affiliation we derive our core beliefs and values and, through them, our sense of who we are, what our life is about, and what meaning attaches to our personal existence.

All this is quite abstract and a bit ethereal, especially when viewed from the outside. In terms of how we actually live our lives, it is background. It is prologue. Our ongoing living centers on something far more concrete, active and tangible.

If I define myself primarily in terms of my political nationality, then my nation-focused actions––such as my willingness to serve in my nation's military forces, paying taxes, voting in elections, or even running for office––define my identity and my personhood. These activities are my contributions to the moral context to which I am affiliated. That context is the moral venue in which I operate. Here I live as a morally active creature. Here my life is defined in terms of my moral contributions within a precise and distinct venue. My contributions to that specific context constitute my personal moral virility.

If I define myself primarily in gender or sexual terms, then my actual sexual activities define my identity and personhood. The particular sexual venue to which I contribute might emphasize monogamy and faithfulness to one sexual partner. Or, it might emphasize aggressively searching for new sexual partners in the course of my daily activities. Or, it might emphasize treating the sexual partner as a mere pawn for my pleasure. Or, it might treat the sexual partner chiefly as an economic asset. Or, it might regard the sexual partner as the destined player for attaining our mutual emotional fulfillment, and so on. In short, the actual content of the sexual venue might vary. But whatever the content, the individual can attain a sense of personal virtue and fulfillment from one's contributions to that venue. It defines and exhibits that individual's moral virility in sexual terms.

Obviously one can consider many more moral contexts that can serve as the primary focus of the participating individual's sense of personal moral virility. The main point in all of these illustrations is that the individual is not just a passive recipient of values and ideals from a social context. On the contrary, the individual sees one's ongoing daily activities as active contributions to that moral context. One makes decisions based on their contribution to that moral context. One evaluates one's actions in such terms as "I am a good American – I pay my taxes," or "I am a good husband – I don't run around after women." The context, the moral venue, is continually nurtured through the ongoing actions by contributing individuals. These actions reiterate and invigorate, through actual deeds by individuals, the content of that venue. And at the same time the contributing individual's sense of personal identity is also continually nurtured and clarified by its having an orienting compass. That compass, that moral context, is the living arena of the individual's identity and sense of moral virility.

In other parts of this book I suggest that moral contexts can be structured so that they totally exclude all other contexts. By affiliating with such a context the individual renounces all other contexts—sometimes, as in the case of religious cult members, even renouncing affiliation with one's own family and moral upbringing. I have called exclusivistic contexts the *local moral universe*. They demand total allegiance from their members. And they tend to receive it—in the form of moral donations that most nonmembers may consider utterly outrageous or evil, but which the true believer regards as entirely appropriate and even sacrosanct.

In such a context, the venue––the moral place from which one operates––may include justifying torture and murder on "moral" grounds. Here, the individual participants may see themselves joyfully contributing to high moral objectives through their murderous deeds. And, as they do so, they see themselves refining and furbishing their own moral identity, dignity and worth as individual human beings. It may sound convoluted and sick, but I am convinced that many SS guards at Auschwitz perceived themselves in precisely such terms. So did many participants in genocide in Bosnia, Kosovo, Rwanda, and Cambodia. They were on a moral crusade, made possible by a distinctive moral venue.

Just what *is* a moral venue? How is a distinctive moral venue developed? Or, more concretely, how could former friends and neighbors suddenly turn on one another murderously, claiming moral justification for their deeds, as happened in Bosnia and Kosovo in the 1990's?

A moral venue rests on a configuration of its moral components. This includes not only a set of values but also a set of priorities among the values. The moral venue may demand absolute and full allegiance to the particular values, as well as the priorities among them. Yet that configuration of values may, itself, constitute a drastically changed version of previous forms of morality and thereby demand entirely new behaviors from the participating individuals.

For example, the Nazis did not ask German physicians to renounce outright their commitment to being healers. But they did manage to convince many physicians––such as the previously mentioned Dr. Wirths––that by accepting the Nazi doctrines they would be contributing to healing the entire German nation. They would become healers in a far more fundamental way. In short, their personal "medical" contribution would count for far more under Nazism than it did before, when they merely treated individual patients.

Similarly, many other components of a distinctive new moral venue are apt to be "reconfigured" versions of previously existing commitments and culture values. This is what makes them acceptable to individuals who can find a way of attaching themselves to that new configuration, seeing it as revitalized versions of their already-existing commitments and values. The new version is particularly beguiling when it promises individuals lives of heightened moral virility.

Yet another ingredient is needed if we are to understand how a Serb would suddenly turn against a Muslim with whom he had been friendly all his life, as actually happened in Bosnia in the 1990's; and how a sensitive and courageous man—a Dr. Wirths, who had secretly treated Jews during the Nazi era – could become an active participant in the extermination of Jews.

The added ingredient is *dormant poison*—like a lingering virus—that can persist in a culture's heritage, even though it is not overt and visible. Sometimes the poison is so inactive that it is not recognized. But it is real, even though it may exist in dormant and inactive form. When activated, it is capable of becoming a catalyst for fundamental reconfiguration of the existing moral venue.

In the case of many German Christians, this meant that in the routines of Christian doctrines there were anti-Semitic components to which they were exposed in the course of their religious education. These components were ordinarily not translated into overt acts of anti-Semitism. They were dormant; they persisted as potential disrupters to the relationships between Christians and Jews. When the situation became ripe—when the dormant poison was activated—it became a catalyst for sudden and extreme outbreaks of anti-Semitic actions.

For example, Adolf Eichmann and Rudolf Hoess (the commandant of Auschwitz) claimed that they were not anti-Semitic, or at least that anti-Semitism was not their primary motivation when they joined the Nazi movement. As that movement turned into a murderous crusade against Jews, these two men became central and lethal operatives of that crusade. I suspect that there may be a small element of truth in their statement that they did not regard themselves as motivated primarily by anti-Semitism. But I also suspect that they had imbibed enough anti-Semitism in the course of their upbringing to be inoculated against seeing Jews as real human beings, and that this remained a dormant component—a poisonous virus—in their makeup. It was available for activation into something ugly and lethal. To begin with, it kept them from saying no when they were asked to participate in their first and possibly relatively minor action against Jews. After that, the momentum took over. They were entrapped in evil and converted into major players in the production of evil. Once their moral zeal was tapped for the murderous cause, it became an awesome, locomotive force, where the dormant virus was amplified a thousand-fold into an out-of-control cancer.

I suspect that, similarly, small ethnic prejudices persisted silently among Balkan Serbs and Croats, even during the forty years after World War II when they coexisted more or less peacefully in Yugoslavia. Their peaceful coexistence obscured the prejudices that were continuing to exist, albeit in dormant form. These could be, and were, reactivated when the political climate changed as the Soviet empire collapsed and Yugoslavia found encouragement for its breakup into separate ethnic enclaves. Then, suddenly, new moral venues were created—under the leadership of political entrepreneurs who had their own non-too-scrupulous agendas—promising new routes to moral virility for the individual who would take up the call to help promote purity for one's particular ethnic community.

The promise of newfound moral virility stands behind the entirely unanticipated zeal for violence against former friends and neighbors. Its roots lie in the very human need to live in a moral universe, with a distinctive moral venue that feeds on one's need for moral meaning in life. Alas, these very human needs can be cruelly subverted when dormant poisons are activated, when moralities are reconfigured, when ordinary human beings are beguiled by new transcending visions for virility in their lives.

Human hunger for meaning and virility feeds on the need of the individual to be attached to a reality that is larger than oneself, thereby transcending one's smallness and vulnerability. It is a way of coping with what would otherwise be a totally lonely existence, an existence that would not be nurtured from an environment. It connects the atomistic individual to an environment. Rephrasing Thomas Hobbes's theme—that life in the raw is nasty, brutish, and short—one can say that existing entirely by and for oneself is existence that is worse than all of these. It is meaningless.

Life devoid of connectivity is devoid of meaning. Meaning requires connectedness. But connectedness is not enough to ensure personal virility, the sense of being alive. It also requires personal contributions to the connected cause. Therein lies the painful possibility that, out of moral zeal for such a cause, an individual may just as readily contribute to horrendous evil as to good. The vehicle for doing each of them, demonstrating the virility of one's connection to a transcending value, is the same.

Constricted Immediacy:
Introduction

In the discussion of cults I already hinted at a constricted immediacy—namely, that the immediate situation in which we can find ourselves may totally exclude everything outside of that situation. It is a closed world. The three following essays make this more explicit. In the essay on the Stanley Milgram experiments I concentrate on the impact of morally constricting the immediacy in which we may find ourselves. The Milgram experiments build on the reality that in our ordinary circumstances we live our lives in the confines of moral contexts. Seeing ourselves contributing to such contexts, we find basic satisfaction, direction and sense of purpose for our lives. Yet a moral context can be so organized that it deliberately excludes the content of other moral contexts. Even the morality of your own upbringing may be ruled out and be defined as a moral context that is totally irrelevant to the context in which you now find yourself. It can happen without extreme coercion but, instead, with persuasiveness based on moral grounds. This is the case in the Milgram experiments.

The Milgram experiments demonstrate a Faustian bargain. The participant gains the freedom to contribute to a moral cause, with its attendant sense of personal satisfaction, accomplishment and fulfillment. But one does so in a particular moral zone, in return for renouncing participation in other moral zones—even renouncing the relevance of the moral injunctions of these other zones of morality. Constricted immediacy has a price.

Fred Emil Katz

In the essay on moral blinding I address another form of constricted immediacy. It consists of the moral blinding we experience when confronted with a situation in which all choices are difficult. I begin the essay by citing the poignant statement by German Protestant theologian Pastor Martin Niemoeller, blaming himself for not standing up for what is right when he first encountered the infringement of that right (Niemoeller eventually spoke out against Hitler and Nazism and was sent to a concentration camp). We sometimes take refuge in focusing on small, immediate issues and ignore the larger issues––telling ourselves that the larger ones are not real, and that, in any case, we shall take control of them in the future. Of course, the cumulative effect of the small decisions may be that the larger issues can no longer be controlled. They can creep up on you in such a way that you can no longer counteract them.

However, moral blinding is not just a matter of passively avoiding conflicting choices. It may include very active steps to achieve not-seeing. Indeed, not-seeing may be developed into an art of its own, including use of one's creative imagination to invent justifications for participating in horrors and avoiding the intrusion of moral criteria one knows only too well.

The essay on moral dilemmas includes the case where an immediately horrifying alternative is chosen because it contributes to a larger good. I describe the latter as the *leader's knowledge dilemma*––illustrated from the haunting possibility that the British city of Coventry was allowed to be bombed by the Germans during World War II. Winston Churchill may have sacrificed the city, knowing it would be bombed, rather than let the Germans know that their secret codes had been broken. Keeping the German military command from knowing that the British had broken the code was regarded as absolutely crucial to having a realistic chance of winning the war. At the time when Churchill would have made this calculation, the war seemed to go entirely in Germany's favor.

Let me hasten to say, however, that I posed a hypothetical situation. No one knows definitively whether or not Churchill had any prior knowledge of the pending Coventry bombing. (There exist contrasting views.) I am using this case merely to illustrate a type of moral dilemma, not as a recitation of historical fact. That dilemma can be put as follows: *One will only be able to continue to know if one does not fully use what one knows.* In a sense,

40

it describes the issue of trust accorded to a psychotherapist, a physician, a consultant: As long as they will limit the use of their knowledge about us, we continue to give them access to knowledge about us. It also describes something about the nature of maturity. Namely, that maturity consists of the prudent uses of knowledge, not the total uses of knowledge. And, finally, it emerges that knowledge is most potent if its use is constricted.

In all the cases cited in the essays of this chapter, immediacy is constricted, and alternatives are discarded or, at least, disregarded.

In all of them the construction of that constricted immediacy requires deliberate action by the participants, at least at the beginning. Afterward the moral constriction of immediacy may acquire a self-escalating momentum of its own––where the external world can be disregarded with seeming moral impunity. Then the Local Moral Universe Prevails.

Fred Emil Katz

A Reassessment of the Milgram Experiments

One of the best-known psychological experiments conducted during the twentieth century was Stanley Milgram's learning experiment. Milgram himself saw it as testing obedience to authority.[1] In looking at these experiments I shall instead focus on how Milgram succeeded in excluding the outside world's morality and, in its place, substituted an entirely different morality in the confines of the laboratory where the experiment took place. This constituted a "constricted" local world, within which entirely immoral behavior (even from the participants' own points of view) could take place.

Similarly, I shall dwell on Christopher Browning's study of German police reservists who became mass murderers (described in his book Ordinary Men).[2] *This, too, will be shown to create a locally constricted world within which formerly unthinkable behavior became thinkable, doable, and, from the participants' points of view, morally justified.*

The emerging issue is the seductive power of such a constricted immediacy. That immediacy combines the exclusion, in ongoing situations, of much of the external world's morality——even the participants' own moral upbringing—— while opening up an entirely new venue for moral behavior within these situations. In that venue participants believe they are making a moral contribution to a morally justified cause. Seduction, indeed.

In the history of twentieth-century psychology, the Milgram experiments stand out as possibly the most imaginative and courageous of all experimental research on human behavior. To be sure there was Ivan Pavlov's even more famous work on conditioning, performed on dogs, and for which he was awarded the Nobel Prize for Physiology and Medicine in 1904. There was the work of numerous other creative and insightful researchers into psychological features of behavior, whose work I cannot even begin to review or cite.

Milgram's experiments stand out because they tough-mindedly addressed an issue that tormented the entire civilized world after the horrors of the Nazi era. That issue was the fact that the citizens of a highly "civilized" nation (modern Germany) had created and actually carried out an organized program of mass brutality that was unmatched in recorded human history. How could this happen? Was it based on something unique to Germany—its culture and upbringing of its citizenry? Were the Germans uniquely prone to obeying authority, as demonstrated in the popular stereotype of Germans, as well as in sophisticated studies of their education and socialization? If so, then presumably Americans would not be so obedience-prone. This is the background to Milgram's experiments designed to test obedience to authority.

Incidentally, when I speak of the Milgram experiments I am actually doing Stanley Milgram an injustice. He did a great deal of creative psychological research aside from his famous work on obedience. For example, long before the era of the Internet and before research on social networks became fashionable, he demonstrated that it required very few intermediaries for an individual to establish personal contact with virtually anyone else (the "small world" possibility). However, in this chapter, I concentrate only on Milgram's experiments on obedience. Here I am following the public awareness of his work. His work on obedience is his most famous work; it is also the most arresting and most deserving of critical reassessment.

Briefly stated, Milgram invited and paid individuals to participate in an experiment that was supposedly concerned with how people remember and learn. At the time Milgram was on the faculty of Yale University. Under the mantle of academic research, with the blessing and sponsorship of that prestigious university, the research was being described to prospective participants.

The actual procedure included an "experimenter," a "learner," and a "subject" (cast in the role of teacher). The exercise consisted of the subject reading a series of paired words and then reading one of the paired words and asking the learner to recall the appropriate matched paired word. The learner was hooked up to an electrical connection. In Milgram's own words, "the subject was told to administer a shock to the learner each time he gave a wrong response. Moreover—and this is the key command—the subject was instructed to 'move one level higher on the shock generator each time the learner gives a wrong answer.' He was also instructed to announce the voltage level before administering a shock. This served to continually remind the subject of the increasing intensity of shocks administered to the learner."[3]

In reality, the electrical connection was fictitious; no shock was actually given. Fictitious, too, were the roles of experimenter and learner. Both were rigged to make it seem that, when the learner (an actor) made mistakes he was actually receiving an electric shock. As the shocks escalated, due to increasing "mistakes" by the pretending learner, he cried out in "agony." But the role of subject was terribly––and terrifyingly––real. He actually believed that he was administering electrical shocks to the inept learner.

The unanticipated and amazing result turned out to be that most subjects were willing to administer electric shocks to the learner. Despite expressing qualms of conscience, most of them kept escalating the level of shock as the learner continued making mistakes, cried out in pain when shocked, and the experimenter continued to tell them that they simply had to continue to follow instructions––the scientific fate of the experiment depended on them doing so.

Milgram carried out this experiment with many different individuals participating as subjects. The experiments were repeated in many different settings, even in different countries. In each of them there were a few exceptions; in Milgram's own laboratory one of those who refused to inflict pain was a woman of German background. The majority of individuals–– ordinary people, not hand-picked sadists––went along with the instructions and were willing to inflict pain on entirely innocent people.

Surely, Milgram rightly maintains, it turns out that obedience to authority––leading to horrendous behavior––was not a uniquely German phenomenon. Quite ordinary people, almost everywhere, seem fully capable of doing such things.

In the post-World War II milieu––where people were still trying to come to grips with the Holocaust and other atrocities––this was not a happy finding. Milgram received his share of opprobrium, to the extent that he sometimes expressed regret that he ever undertook this work. Yet, scientifically and objectively, there seems little doubt that his findings stand up and must be taken seriously.

In recent years there have been many other indications that "ordinary people" are quite willing to take part in horrendous activities. All of these findings are indebted to Milgram's work. His findings are being borne out again and again (a little later I shall take up a prominent example, provided by the work of Christopher Browning). Yet the mind still boggles at the idea of ordinary people–– who are not sick or demented––doing horrendous things to others. Factually we know that this happens. Intellectually, we are still bewildered. For this reason it is necessary to dig a little more deeply into Milgram's experiments.

First of all, the Milgram experiments––just as any other scientific work––operates under the auspices of a particular paradigm. A paradigm, as Thomas Kuhn taught us, is a particular framework, in a particular era, under which a particular science operates at that time.[4] Reigning paradigms organize the perspective, the focus of attention that is deemed to legitimately need the scientist's attention. Not only do they specify which issues need attention, which problems are worthy of attack, but they specify which means are legitimately used––which research methodology is legitimate and which is not legitimate. In short, they specify how the scientist looks at and approaches the world. Yet paradigms also include blinders. They rule out as well as rule in––mysticism, for example, is typically ruled out. The blinders need to concern us.

In the Milgram experiments one can detect three different paradigms. There is the paradigm that governs Milgram's own perspective as he goes about designing and carrying out the experiments. There is the paradigm used to persuade the subjects to participate in the experiment; it is not identical with Milgram's own. Third, there is a paradigm I propose for understanding Milgram's experiments––an outsider's paradigm.

Milgram's paradigm for his own work, as he sees it, is focused on experimentally studying how individuals obey authority––and creating the psychological climate where obedience can be studied in a specially contrived laboratory situation. Laboratory contrivings–– where there is deliberate manipulation of the ways in which research subjects interact with one another in a controlled situation––have a substantial history and standing in the field of psychology. They include studies using animals or humans as subjects. The latter, as in the experiments carried out by Gestalt psychologists manipulates the setting in which people make judgments and decisions, so that specific variables can be controlled and assessed. Typically, the experimenter tries to test for a few crucial factors while deliberately excluding the intrusion of other factors. Milgram's experiments fall within this tradition, this paradigm.

The paradigm Milgram used to persuade the subjects focuses on the need to understand the process of learning and remembering. It highlights the need to address such matters in scientific ways, where science may require difficult adjustments in one's own behavior; where one's contribution to science is a major and honorable contribution to the world, even if one is just a lowly participant in an experiment. To achieve these scientifically honorable ends it is absolutely crucial that one obeys the instructions of the experimenter to the letter, even if one finds them difficult. One thereby does credit to participation in the world of science; one is personally making a contribution to that world.

The paradigm I am proposing is that, through his various psychological manipulations, Milgram created a distinctive local moral universe in the laboratory in which the experiment took place. It consisted of creating a distinct moral context for the participating individuals, the "subjects." Here, their external world––their home life, their personal upbringing, their various other affiliations and allegiances––were declared to be out of bounds, irrelevant, and inappropriate. They were told that here, in the laboratory, was a system of morality that fully governed what went on. It was a distinctive and complete moral system. It must be adhered to in order to achieve the very noble ends of the scientific experiment. Here, the moral universe of the subjects was constricted by the locally created moral order in which they found themselves. A moral myopia prevailed.

To be sure, individual participants occasionally tried to bring in their outside values. Each time this happened these concerns were decisively and totally overruled by the experimenter.

The striking thing is how successful Milgram was in creating such a Local Moral Universe. There is no indication that he deliberately intended to create one. But, nonetheless, he seems to have succeeded in doing so.

In the history of science it is not at all unusual for different paradigms to be applied to the same data. My proposing to substitute a different paradigm for Milgram's does not lessen the originality and brilliance of his work. It does mean, however, that an outsider has the benefit of operating from a different reference point and thereby has the option to operate with a different paradigm.

The difference between Milgram's paradigm and mine is nowhere more explicit than their application to the notorious My Lai massacre. At My Lai, a small village in Vietnam, several hundred unarmed civilians were killed by American soldiers one day. That event aroused wide reaction, including many efforts by scholars to try to understand how this could have happened. Milgram's explanation, with its focus on obedience to authority, emphasized that the participating soldiers, in their obedience to authority, utterly abandoned their moral responsibilities, becoming virtual automatons, who acted thoughtlessly.[5]

By contrast, I suggest that the soldiers at My Lai had switched into a distinctive and new, locally generated moral context. In that context they operated within distinctive rules, distinctive rewards were at hand, distinctive aspirations were at work, and distinctive kinds of options were exercised. Far from being automatons, the soldiers acted with zeal and joy and, even, creativity. They felt they were doing the right thing (which Milgram himself cites"). They were operating in the confines of a Local Moral Universe. The content of their "morality" strikes us as appalling. But, in its own perverse way, theirs was indeed a system of morality. (I have discussed this more fully in the book *Ordinary People and Extraordinary Evil.*)

Returning to the Milgram experiments, one must note that each paradigm has distinctive linkages to an outside reality, distinctive options of its own, and distinctive blinders. All of these are facilitated by what I have been calling *riders*, a pervading point of view that overlays one's reality, giving it a distinctive coloration as well as linkage to particular sectors of the external world.

In the case of Milgram's own paradigm, this includes a rider of awareness—and thereby linkage into the experiment—of the horrors perpetrated by Germany under the Nazi regime. Here was an extremely authoritarian government and a country where authority was worshipped in extreme fashion. Surely, obedience to authority must be more fully understood. Perhaps it will present us with a clue as to how so much suffering could be created in our own time and perhaps prevented in the future. In the personal case of Milgram, that suffering had victimized his fellow Jews most of all. Deception seemed justified as an option in one's search, even if it involved blinders to some venerable moral issues, such as both lying to the subjects and persuading them to engage in immoral acts. After all, one's research was addressing fundamental aspects of human behavior. From this knowledge, perhaps one could prevent another Holocaust?

In the paradigm Milgram bestowed onto the subjects, the rider consisted of one's linkage––however fleetingly––to the prestige of a university and to the world of science. It provided the option of doing things one would ordinarily not do. It served as blinders to actively engaging one's own moral standards. All this took place while one believed one had joined, temporarily to be sure, the community of scientists.

In the local moral universe paradigm I am advocating there is a rider comprised of the notion that humans are fundamentally moral creatures. We get our sense of who we are from perceiving that we are linked to a larger moral context. Moreover, we attain a sense of our personal moral virility from actually making a contribution to that moral context. Within that context we see our options. From this comes the seductiveness of a moral context. When offered a moral context, and the opportunity to participate in it, we envision the rewards derived from our own contributions. We are, after all, about to enrich the moral universe to which we subscribe.

The Milgram subjects were made to feel that they were making a moral contribution to a moral context. They were embraced by a deliberately created context. Through it they became personally linked, in their own mind, to the pursuit of larger moral goals. Through their own contribution to that pursuit, they were exercising moral virility. To be sure, they bought this at a price––namely, the exercise of blinders to their external moral upbringing. Instead, they were exercising their option to contribute to something they had come to regard as noble and important.

Milgram reports that the subjects were occasionally feeling and expressing extreme discomfort about inflicting electric shocks on the learner. Yet they continued to inflict them. Here is an example: A subject tells the experimenter––"He [the learner] can't stand it. I'm not going to kill that man in there. You hear him hollering in there. He's hollering. He can't stand it."[7] The subject is desperately wanting to stop administering shocks, but he continues to do so. Clearly, there is a binding constraint on him not based on physical force; no one is physically forcing him to continue. It is a moral force, a binding moral bond. A moral community has come into existence locally in the laboratory. There, any deviation is seen as a moral transgression[8]; one would be breaking one's moral obligations if one stopped administering electric shocks to the screaming learner.

In this local moral community very distinctive obligations prevail. These are kept going by the explicit directions given by the experimenter—telling the subject that he simply must continue to administer shocks, regardless of the obvious anguish and pain of the learner. They are also kept going by a situational etiquette (this is Milgram's term, based on the work of Erving Goffman) where, in the confines of an ongoing situation it becomes increasingly difficult to change one's behavior. The subject has promised to follow instructions. One cannot lightly break a promise, an obligation to the experimenter personally and to the entire program. One is bound, socially and morally. Such values as loyalty, dependability, and honesty are invoked to keep one in line. One is, in short, a member of a moral community—based on moral bonding among its members—where in return for moral rewards there are also distinctive moral obligations. In the immediate situation there are moral bindings that accompany moral bonding.

The above example of subjects expressing discomfort about inflicting pain on an innocent person should not deflect us from realizing that the majority of Milgram's subjects completed their participation in the experiment with the feeling that they had contributed to important work. They were satisfied with their participation. They felt that their activity in the experiment was entirely worthwhile. Although they did not use quite these terms, they indicated that they felt that what they did was morally justified.

In a larger sense, a Local Moral Universe asserts itself by shutting out the moral authority of anything outside its own boundaries. It becomes blind to competing moralities. But, in exchange, it offers its own adherents a wealth of options to enhance and celebrate their moral virility, provided they do so within the confines of the proffered moral universe. In this manner, that constricted world fills the immediacy of their existence.

One must not assume that in the Local Moral Universe, as it is exemplified in the Milgram experiments, the values of the outside world are totally and magically excluded. More accurately, when they are allowed to enter they are likely to be subverted through repackaging. As already mentioned, many subjects in the experiment retained great misgivings about shocking innocent people; their outside values were still real to them. Yet, they told themselves, "they could not muster the inner resources to translate their values into action."[9]

Subjects felt bound by the system. Still, given their misgivings, some "derived satisfaction from their [negative] thoughts and felt that––within themselves, at least––they had been on the side of the angels."[10] In short, they were using their own discretion to manufacture a rationalization for their own participation in the system. They did so by acknowledging their outside values, though in a most convoluted form. In a way, they were thereby making the horror system work. By repackaging their outside values in such a way that they could continue to live with themselves while engaging in behavior that was diametrically opposed to their values, they were turning these values into an instrument for supporting the system of horror.

Of course the experimenter was also willing to invoke outside values–– such as loyalty, dependability, and honesty––to ensure the continuation of the horrors; here, too, there was repackaging of values. In short, outside values were indeed allowed to intrude into the Local Moral Universe of the Milgram experiments. But they did so in a highly selective way; they were repackaged through the machinations of the experimenter and the inadvertent collusion of the subjects. In this way the Local Moral Universe imprinted its distinctive character.

Next, let us turn to Browning's report on harrowing human behavior that is somewhat in keeping with Milgram's findings. But in contrast to Milgram's artificially contrived laboratory situation, Browning provides a report on events that actually occurred. The events occurred in the Nazi era in Poland.

Browning describes the actions of a battalion of German police reservists, based in Hamburg, who had hoped to sit out the war without having to engage in combat. They were somewhat older than the average soldier; they had respected places in their community, stable occupations, and families. They were not young fanatics. Few were Nazi Party members.

Eventually, this battalion of approximately five hundred men was activated for military duty and sent to Poland. On arrival there, the battalion was assigned the task of carrying out mass exterminations of Jews––killing these innocent people who inhabited villages in the region around the town of Lublin. Initially, individual members of the battalion were given the option not to participate, but virtually all of them did. In the course of sixteen months, some tried to distance themselves from the killings. But the majority––Browning estimates between eighty and ninety percent––went ahead and carried out the killings. Some did so with reluctance; some did so with zeal. Most of them merely complied. With these findings Browning guides us into a terrifying world: Ordinary people––people we cannot readily write off as sadists, poisoned anti-Semites, or ethnic zealots––could and did engage in mass killings of innocent people.

Although I have been wrestling with this same issue for some years, and have even published a book on it,[11] I have great difficulty citing and addressing Browning's revelations. The area of Poland to which the police reservists were sent in June 1942 and where they carried out their activities is the vicinity to which my own father and mother and all other remaining Jews from my German village were sent in April 1942. They died there, at Izbica. My older brother, having emigrated to Holland and captured by the invading Germans, was also sent there; he died at Sobibor. Even though Browning does not specifically mention my loved ones, he describes their fate. With their memory in mind and my obligation to them, I undertake the distasteful task of building on Browning's work.

Browning ends his report with the statement that "one comes away from the story of Reserve Battalion 101 with great unease." I take this to mean that he feels great unease not only about the nature of the horrors he has reported but also about the inadequacy of existing explanations as to how such things can happen. He summarizes these existing explanations–– such as the Milgram experiments––expertly and fully. Yet they leave him, and surely all of us, with a sense that we are still disconcertingly short of really convincing and adequate explanations.

I come to Browning's depictions from the conviction that even such horrors as he describes are not entirely beyond our capacity to comprehend. We need to create, and we can create the appropriate conceptual tools, the ways of looking so that we may see more clearly. By seeing more clearly we may eventually create effective weapons against such horrors.

First and foremost, the members of Police Battalion 101 were molded into a cohesive moral community. This was achieved by their common training and association with one another before they left Hamburg; by their relatively constant membership in the battalion; and, above all, by being removed, together, from their home setting––to the Lublin section of Poland––where they formed an enclave of their own, physically separated from their home and culturally loosened from many of their home constraints. It was their first field assignment; here, a new moral community could and did flourish. It developed its own local system of community––its system of where each man fits. The duties and obligations of soldiers to one another can override many more abstract notions of morality, as it does for many military units actively engaged in combat. Here immediacy prevails. It does so in the form of new, locally generated standards of morality, loyalty, and decency.

For example, Browning reports that when it was one's obligation to become a shooter––a killer in a very explicit way––then those who were still appalled by this role and who tried to evade it, tended to explain their reluctance to shoot as their own "weakness," rather than moral degeneracy of that "obligation." In short, even these "deviants" were upholding the local morality, in which it was supposedly one's obligation––one's moral obligation––to shoot designated people. Often the reluctant shooters were told by their comrades that shooting was everyone's obligation. By not shooting they were doing damage to the whole unit. They were evading their personal obligation to the group and its mission.

One's carrying out this obligation underscored one's good standing in this community––as a good soldier, who can be counted on to do his share of the task. It also added to one's own stature. Precisely because it was onerous, one was making a noble contribution, demonstrating moral virility. It was but a short step to demonstrating zeal in the fine art of killing. Even those who began with moral scruples against personally carrying out killings could become proficient and no longer reluctant. They were drawn into a system with its own set of rewards. Being regarded as a good soldier is about as high an honor as you can possibly hope to achieve in the confines of this Local Moral Universe. One's killings could be carried out without anesthetizing liquor. One can come to enjoy killing.

Even those who did not become zealots tended to accept the obligation––
to kill designated people––on moral grounds.

There was room for different forms of participation. Browning reports
that there "emerged within Reserve Battalion 101: a nucleus of increasingly
enthusiastic killers who volunteered for the firing squads and 'Jew hunts';
a larger group . . . who performed as shooters and ghetto clearers when
assigned but who did not seek opportunities to kill (and in some cases
refrained from killing, contrary to standing orders, when no one was
monitoring their actions); and a small group (less than twenty percent) of
refusers and evaders."[12] But even the latter, as I mentioned earlier, tended to
classify themselves as weaklings, thereby honoring the prevailing morality
in their military unit.

At the heart of the tragedy is that the majority of participants came
to regard their actions as morally justified, at least at the time of their
participation. The rest of us, living in a very different moral milieu, find
this appalling. But our reaction must not blind us. The reality is that we
are all moral creatures. We require a moral context for our own sense of
who and what we are. By our own active contribution to that context, we
create our sense of personal virility, our sense of being alive and worthy of
being alive. All this is normal and "ordinary."

What is distinctive in the police battalion's actions in Poland is that
it constitutes a particular moral mutation––a locally evolving system of
morality with locally tinged priorities grafted onto the past and the larger
society. Its emerging culture––its values and morality, its customs––
contains highly localized coloration of the immediacy in which it exists.
Moral mutations such as these are not unusual. They arise from particular
circumstances at hand; in this case, the battalion's assignment to active
duty and being sent to Poland. They address particular issues immediately
at hand; in this case, being assigned the task of murdering entire segments
of the Jewish population. They make use of the particular resources at
hand; in this case, molding themselves into a community that will actually
carry out the assignment and do so by harnessing entirely normal human
attributes, such as those of gearing one's moral virility to the task at hand.
They thereby create a new moral configuration, one that is permeated by
a locally generated, constricted vision of the world, where a morality can

come to prevail that is utterly and entirely at variance with the outside world from which the participants come. A Local Moral Universe prevails.

If one were to restrict oneself to the Milgram orientation, one might be inclined to say that, as good Germans, these police reservists were simply obeying orders. Yet I would say that a more persuasive view is that these men, just as the subjects in Milgram's experiments, developed and operated within a distinctive Local Moral Universe. It nurtured a singularly constricted moral vision among them.

The most fundamental lesson one must learn is that social contexts can be created where individuals––who are not morally depraved to begin with, who are not sick in any clinical sense, who are not deviants or social misfits––can do horrendous deeds. They are not just being brainwashed, coerced, or seduced into obeying unquestioningly. On the contrary, there can be created such constricted immediacies so that individuals will gladly, willingly and "morally" engage in horrors.

The seduction comes from the fact that contexts offer themselves as venues for effective moral living, for personal fulfillment, for reaching out to life itself. The discussion in this chapter––with its focus on the creation and operation of what I am calling the Local Moral Universe–– has tried to show how this process works. I hope that analysis of the Local Moral Universe––be it the one in Milgram's laboratory or in the real world––can eventually give us weapons against such horrors. After all, they show us how the recruitment process works; how the enforcement process works; how ordinary people can be transformed into willing and active participants.

The lesson, I hope, is that once we recognize how this process works, we will not so easily become its unwitting partners.

NOTE

1 Stanley Milgram, *Obedience to Authority: An Experimental View* (New York: Harper and Row, 1974).
2 Christopher Browning, *Ordinary Men: Reserve Battalion 101 and the Final Solution in Poland* (New York: Harper Perennial, 1993).
3 Milgram, *Obedience to Authority,* pp. 20-21.
4 Thomas S. Kuhn, *The Structure of Scientific Revolutions* (Chicago: University of Chicago Press, 1962).
5 "Epilogue," Milgram, *Obedience to Authority.*
6 Ibid., p. 185.
7 Ibid., p. 148.
8 Milgram himself uses this term. He follows the formulation of Erving Goffman in his book, *The Presentation of Self in Everyday Life* (New York: Doubleday Anchor Books, 1959). My use of the term differs somewhat from theirs. They focus on how the individual feels the moral constraint on one's sense of self.
9 Milgram, *Obedience to Authority*, p. 10.
10 Ibid. The commandant of Auschwitz, Rudolf Hoess, made a somewhat similar claim. He reported that he felt appalled by some of the things that took place at Auschwitz under his own command. But feeling appalled made him believe that he was still a human being. Hence, of course, he need not commit suicide or even radically change the system he was commanding. Being appalled––that is, bringing in some humane values––could be so twisted, so repackaged, that it served to make the horror system continue to operate.
11 Fred Emil Katz, *Ordinary People and Extraordinary Evil: A Report on the Beguilings of Evil* (Albany, NY: State University of New York Press, 1993).
12 Browning, op.cit., p. 168.

Blindings Against Immediacy:
Some Moral Games We Play When We Confront Unpleasant Realities

> *One of the most often cited insights about the Holocaust is the following statement by Martin Niemoeller, a German Protestant minister, speaking about the Nazi era: "First they came for the socialists, and I did not speak out––because I was not a socialist. Then they came for the trade-unionists and I did not speak out––because I was not a trade-unionist. Then they came for the Jews, and I did not speak out––because I was not a Jew. Then they came for me––and there was no one left to speak for me."*
>
> *Leonard Baker, a biographer of Rabbi Leo Baeck, the leader of Germany's Jewish community during the Nazi era, writes about the reactions of German Jews to their escalating persecution by the Nazis: "They could not believe it. They could not believe they would be stripped of their citizenship until it happened. They could not believe their houses of worship would be destroyed until it happened. They could not believe they would be torn from their homes and families until it happened. And now they could not believe they would be murdered."[1]*

Both of the above quotes illustrate severe forms of blinding and moral numbing in the face of reality that cries out to be looked at, seen for what it is, and confronted. Behind the blinding and moral numbing is the sheer physical and psychological necessity of not permitting our neural system to be overloaded. Consider the huge number of stimuli that hit us each and every minute of our waking day (and, for that matter, in our sleep as well). It is entirely normal and necessary that human beings not react to every single stimulus that comes our way.

If, on any given day, we responded to each and every stimulus that has a bearing on our life, we might not live out that day. Surely one of the hallmarks of a number of mental illnesses is that the individual is overly responsive to stimuli––one cannot weigh stimuli and relegate some to the background as not needing an immediate response. We must restrict our reactions in order to function, even for a single day. In sheer self-defense against being overloaded with stimuli––and dissipating our strengths to the point of exhaustion and self-destruction––we must, of necessity, limit our reactions. As a result, we are habituated to not reacting, to dismissing most stimuli that come our way. It becomes quite easy and routine to do so. It is entirely normal and necessary.

Therein lies a danger. We can become callous to monstrosity. We can do so not because we are attracted to monstrosity or condone it, but because we have, at hand, ready ways of not-confronting.

Ways of not-confronting are easily and habitually utilized. They give us the tools to avoid addressing moral monstrosities, just as they give us the tools to avoid routine over-stimulation. From this comes perhaps the most common moral danger that afflicts us. People who deliberately accept and embrace moral monstrosities are probably few in number. Far more common are people who can avoid confronting issues of moral monstrosities by making use of very readily available ways of acting routinely, the same ways they use much of the time in the course of their mundane daily living. These include the dismissal, most of the time, of uncomfortable stimuli.

Toward extreme danger facing ourselves we can become frozen and disoriented, while looking for a way out by concentrating on a small, dismissible component part. To unpleasant events that do not affect us personally––to unfair practices, to death and torture, to the enslavement of other people––we can easily and customarily turn a deaf ear. Here, too, we may conveniently concentrate on the dismissible part––it does not really affect us personally

Commonly dilemmas arise in which we find ourselves in a situation that may contain upsetting or bewildering items, among which no good choice exists. We may have choices, but all of them are woeful. We then make efforts to do the least woeful thing, to keep from seeing what we are seeing. We cannot stand being blinded.

In all of the above, our response is apt to go beyond passively not seeing. It may include very active not-seeing. This can, in turn, produce horrific results in the immediacy of our lives. It may all begin in an initial misjudgment––as illustrated by Pastor Niemoller's first misjudgment--which, seemingly, is confined to a small, local, immediate issue. But a small, seemingly local decision by an individual may set in motion the momentum for a cumulative process of increasingly grotesque moral aberrations to which that individual actively contributes or, at least, acquiesces.

Each act of unresponsiveness is indeed an act. Not responding is a form of response. As Pastor Niemoeller's statement illustrates for us, by not responding to a specific assault on our sensibility we may thereby lay the groundwork for not responding the next time, and the next time after that. We are creating a pattern of callousness that has its own internal momentum. It becomes more difficult to break the momentum of ever-more callous actions, making it increasingly easy to act callously when a new challenge presents itself.

Technically, what happens is that each act of callousness becomes a rider to the next occasion when we are called on to react. It overlays that next situation in the form of a precedent that established a mode of response for the new occasion and, in all likelihood, will determine the direction of that next response. This will apply even when the next situation supplies us with ever-more extreme challenges. Indeed, it is precisely the preexisting "directionality" of response already in our repertoire that makes the more extreme challenge bearable and acceptable. The extreme becomes routine because it is not a total aberration from the past.

Non-responsiveness to individual acts of abomination can, then, become part of an escalating process that eventually denies the capacity to react to even the most drastic and bizarre challenges to our moral conscience. We become immobilized from acting flexibly and appropriately; we are morally fossilized. Our past actions have destroyed our capacity to remain humane, to respond to new assaults on humane concerns.

This applies to both the perpetrators and victims of the horrors. An extreme version of the latter are the *Musselmaenner,* the living dead in the concentration camps, who have renounced all life and are death-bound in part, at least, through their own total renunciation of any life-affirming responses to what confronts them.

Stated a bit more theoretically, we can become locked into a self-perpetuating process of escalating estrangement from our own initial moral moorings. A new "morality" is being created through our own actions (this, too, applies to the *Musselman*, who has arrived at a morality of total meaninglessness of life and who actively, through his behavior, contributes to making that morality a reality), it may begin in a seemingly small, inconsequential act. It then evolves its own internal dynamics of ever-more extreme actions that dominates the immediacy of one's life.

This process tends to be augmented by our efforts to justify our course of action by producing some sort of justification——usually an attempt at moral justification——for living with ourselves while engaged in a particular course of action. This is another dimension of the process of blinding. I now turn to it.

Instead of apparent non-responsiveness to unpleasant realities, we sometimes provide very active responses. These active responses may consist of creating an imaginary scenario, one that thoroughly distorts reality, one that enables one to accept reality only in an illusory version. Here it is, in the form of statements made by two German citizens, being interviewed some five years after World War II. One of them states: "We won *both* [the First and Second World] wars, and *both* times we were betrayed."[2]

In fact, Germany lost both world wars. Who betrayed whom? Those who actually won these wars? Those German officials who surrendered to the victorious Allies and accepted a peace treaty? Those who accepted reality and expected their fellow citizens to adapt to that reality? Or, perhaps, the betrayers are some sort of amorphous, floating band of enemies——Jews, Communists, homosexuals and others yet to be named whenever the need arises to conveniently blame someone for troubles one cannot seem to resolve.

Another German citizen, interviewed at about the same time, says, in reference to the two World Wars: "Twice we have had to fight the whole world, all alone . . . what good are the Italians or the Japanese?"[3]

As the man himself admits, Germany did have allies. She did not fight alone; Italy and Japan were active allies of Germany, fighting the Allied armies (although, admittedly, the Italian armies were not as effective as the German armies; but this was certainly not true for the Japanese armies). But more glaringly fictitious is the claim that Germany "had to fight"——when the rest of the world and some people within Germany itself——realized that it was German adventurism that *initiated* these wars. Both responses indicate that even in a most beleaguered situation——with seemingly incontrovertible evidence of individuals being responsible for horrendous deeds––these individuals still have a measure of autonomy to invent stories so that they can live with themselves. They can find a way to blind themselves.

Let us consider Dr. Eduard Wirths again, whom I discuss at various points in this book.[4] Dr. Wirths created ways to keep from being blinded by the horrors in which he was participating very fully at Auschwitz. His method was to create the fiction that by going along with the horrors, he was helping to produce a better future–– not only for the German nation but for his own wife and their children, whom he loved most dearly. In ardent letters to his wife, written while he was at Auschwitz, he told her various versions of the fiction that, despite the horrors in which he was engaged, he was actively working toward a better life of their family, particularly for their children. He was thereby keeping himself from being blinded by the horrors in which he personally participated. He did so by creating a new moral formula, one he could live with. Unfortunately this meant that he was able to keep doing what he was doing; he had manufactured a moral justification. He was no longer seeing what was to be seen––and this by a man who had previously been unusually courageous and sensitive to the moral teachings most Westerners would recognize and applaud!

In the above examples we see blindings being buttressed by elaborate rationalizations and distortions. We see total inversion of historical and contemporary reality. We see active myth making. All these activities keep individuals from seeing what is to be seen. And, by not seeing, perpetrators of evil can justify to themselves that their horrendous course of action is entirely justified. They can live with their conscience while participating in horrific activities.

They do so by using their autonomy to manufacture moral justification for their deeds. They make their house of horrors seem to have a moral basement. They live in that house. Within it there is no place for uncertainty, doubt and moral dilemma. Theirs is not the world of Pastor Niemoeller, who lives in a house of crushing moral guilt and uncertainty. No, theirs is a world of false moral rectitude. To produce it they have built a house upon gravestones.

NOTE

1 Leonard Baker, *Days of Sorrow and Pain: Leo Baeck and the Berlin Jews* (New York, Macmillan, 1978), p. 273.

2 Milton Mayer, *They Thought They Were Free: The Germans, 1933-45* (Chicago: University of Chicago Press, 1971), p. 258.

3 Ibid.

4 Based on the case study of Dr. Wirths conducted by Robert J. Lifton, reported in his book, *The Nazi Doctors: Medical Killing and the Psychology of Genocide* (New York: Basic Books, 1986).

Moral Dilemmas in Immediacy:
Knowing Too Little, Knowing Too Much

"Tell me now––how was the world lost?... The world was lost in 1935, here in Germany. It was I who lost it, and I will tell you how."[1]

These are the words of a conscience-stricken German man, interviewed about five years after World War II by an American (Jewish) reporter. The man relates how, in 1935, he was ordered to take an oath of allegiance to the Nazis in order to retain his job and ensure some measure of economic security for his family. He pondered for a day, then took the oath––telling himself that by joining the Nazis he might be able to save some endangered people by operating from within the Nazi system.

At the time of the interview he believed that, by taking the oath of allegiance to the Nazis, he made an infinitely immoral decision. In the German culture an oath of allegiance is an extremely binding act; he had bound himself to Nazism. He now believes that if he had refused, thousands of others would also have refused, and this would have led to the downfall of the Nazis; that his taking the oath was an evil act, an active step of committing evil.

He says that at the time when he took the oath, his faith failed him; "If my faith had been strong enough in 1935, I could have prevented the whole evil . . . I did not believe that I could 'move mountains' . . . my faith failed me. So, in the next years, I was able to remove only anthills, not mountains."[2] He actually saved some people, but not as many as he wished he had.

A simplistic assessment of this man's action in 1935 is that he took only the immediate issues into consideration––chiefly, the importance of keeping his job and feeding his family––rather than the larger picture, especially the larger consequences of his action. Doubtless, many people who joined the Nazi party did so from precisely such "localized" considerations, where one's immediate needs are paramount and the long-term consequences are not given serious consideration.

Many of us find ourselves in occupational careers as the result of such immediacy-focused, localized decisions. These local decisions can become cumulative—each one becomes an increment in a larger career process, where the endpoint may never have been planned or even seriously considered, but where a series of local decisions create a distinctive trajectory that becomes irreversible. In terms of how one makes career decisions, the German man may not be so different from the rest of us.

The man thought that in 1935 he was taking larger issues into consideration. But he was surely seduced by the present, by the immediate issues he confronted, into not giving enough weight to any voice of doubt within himself; in contrast, he was giving great weight to the very real issue of his job security and his family's financial well-being. And the little voice within was weak and unclear.

To be sure the future was blurred; the man could not possibly know the degree of horror the Nazis would eventually produce—and how his own actions might contribute. As Yogi Berra might say, the future is in the future; we'll know the future in the future—and only then.

When the man speaks of not having had enough faith, is he saying that even when one does not know just what will happen, one ought to nonetheless trust one's intuitive inklings? Should one do so even when the inklings go counter to immediate pressures that contain tangible, current benefits? Should one make no compromises, ever? When does one know one is about to take an evil step? When do one's vague doubts and apprehensions turn out to be profoundly true?

Surely, among the pressures of immediacy, one is in the throes of moral dilemmas compounded by knowledge discrepancy: The relatively certain knowledge of issues in the immediacy as against the vague knowledge of possible dangers in the future.

The German man's hindsight-driven belief is that if he had refused to take the Nazi oath he would, then, have become the catalyst for thousands of others to make a similar refusal and that this, in turn, might have led to the downfall of Nazism.

Let us recall that when the Nazi murders of mentally defective children became known, in the 1930s, there was a public outcry. As a result the Nazis stopped the program. Again, there was an occasion, in Berlin, when the Christian wives of Jewish men organized mass demonstrations against their husbands' arrests. They took to the streets of Berlin and loudly made their outrage known. Thereupon the men were released. In both cases we learn that when knowledge is harnessed it can become an effective weapon, even against a tyrannical regime. Perhaps the same result would have been achieved if the persecution of Jews had met with a public outcry––catalyzed by such actions as the German man's hindsight-driven "refusal" to take an oath of allegiance to the Nazis.

Yes, through his oath of allegiance the German man accepted––and collaborated with––the reigning national hypocrisy of Nazi Germany. But don't all of us accept hypocrisies much of the time? During World War II the citizens of Allied countries accepted the need to win that war, even if meant obliterating entire cities. To be sure, in the immediacy of the beginning of that war, the Nazis unleashed mass bombings of civilians, giving the Allies precedent for adding their own version later on in that war. The immediacy of that war––and most wars––seduces the citizenry into increasing acceptance of mass slaughter of innocent people. In the climate of looking for monsters––on the "other side"––it becomes increasingly difficult to effectively harness knowledge about the victims. (Among "innocent" people I include, here, the conscripted soldiers, on both sides, who, ordered to serve in wars, are basically innocent at the start before becoming their country's assigned killers who, then, often perform their gruesome "duty" with acquired fervor, alacrity, tenacity, and skill.)

From World War II we remember Coventry, Dresden, Hiroshima, and Nagasaki––all largely civilian cities that were suddenly and largely destroyed by an aerial bombing. The early German indiscriminate air attacks on civilian targets established this precedent. They made the unthinkable thinkable––and doable––with rarely a murmur of public dissent by the perpetrating power's citizenry. National hypocrisies tend to be implemented in immediacy-driven actions that can become increasingly severe, increasingly evil––if we define evil as the deliberate killing or maiming of innocent people. What is morally most disturbing, the actions become increasingly immune to criticism through application of knowledge that might discredit the horrifying actions. The actions gain an internal, self-escalating dynamic, which, most frighteningly, is governed by its own local system of morality (what I have been calling the Local Moral Universe) that can no longer be penetrated by an external morality.

Here a particular morally constricted immediacy is master. It fuels the fires by permitting only highly selective uses of knowledge while barring uncomfortable knowledge. I have been talking about moral issues in rather general terms of knowledge harnessing and knowledge barring. Let us now look at a more down-to-earth but still hypothetical issue.

The Leader's Knowledge Dilemma

The German bombing of the British city of Coventry during World War II contains a particularly stark dilemma, at least hypothetically. British scientists had finally broken the secret code used by the German war leaders to communicate among themselves and their armed forces. It discussed such items as the dispatch of military units to specific regions and how these units were to be deployed and activated. It covered military plans for the future as well as ones that were actually being implemented. This information enabled the British leaders to know the size and focus of the German military actions, as well as the names of leaders in charge of the respective operations. Most importantly, it enabled the British leaders to know much of what the German military leaders were planning to do *before* these plans were actually carried out.

It was never fully established whether, in fact, Winston Churchill knew ahead of time that Coventry was going to be bombed. What I am here calling "the leader's knowledge dilemma" is strictly a hypothetical statement in this particular case, based on the assumption that he may well have known.

Britain had to keep its knowledge of the German code a secret, lest the Germans change the system and, thereby, deprive Britain of this vital form of information. Based on being able to tap into the German plan to bomb the city of Coventry––with a massive air raid that would certainly kill many, perhaps thousands, of citizens of Coventry––Churchill (if he knew) was faced with a dilemma. If he acted on this information by reinforcing Coventry's defense, the Germans would realize that the British had somehow gained access to their communication system and secret codes. They would immediately change their code system––which, until then, they had assumed to be impenetrable and, therefore, had entrusted it with carrying the most vital secrets of the German war effort. This would deprive the British leaders of the one major advantage they had over the rampaging German war machine. Churchill's (hypothetical) dilemma was, is the certain death of thousands of innocent British citizens worth the price of keeping the secret that Britain had access to Germany's secret codes? Was his decision swayed by military considerations––that winning the war required making the human sacrifice of thousands of his fellow citizens? Here the long-term objective outweighed the short-term price–– although, to the victims and their families, the price was terribly long-term; it was permanent and ultimate. For Churchill, his capacity to function as leader of the British war effort depended on his ability to ignore––or at least strictly limit his concern with––this side of the picture, namely the immediacy as experienced by the victims and their families. The issue is somewhat similar to the dilemma faced by the military general whose own son serves in one of the units under his command, and where that unit is sent on a suicide mission.

In this hypothetical situation, what would have happened to Churchill, personally and politically, if it had become publicly known that he had actually sacrificed Coventry? How might he have acted if a close relative of his had been living in Coventry––might this have introduced a new item into his personal immediacy? As to timing: Suppose it became known to the mayor of Coventry, *before* the actual attack on Coventry, that Churchill held the key to the city's survival? Presumably Churchill's fortunes––his ability to function, to make decisions––depended on keeping the dilemma secret from his own citizens. Most especially, it depended on his capacity to strictly focus on what he regarded as the long-term goal.

Another twist: How important is it––to us, here and now––to resolve whether, in fact, Churchill knew anything about the pending raid? For the sake of the intellectual exercise about the inherent moral dilemma when choice is difficult, it may not be terribly important to do so. We are here dealing with a thought experiment–– Albert Einstein's favorite technique for clarifying and digging into a scientific issue. On the other hand, in terms of practical realities––of life as it is actually lived––it seems terribly important to know whether Churchill knew.

We live in an age where knowledge is increasingly the primary form of power. For all of us there is the issue of access to knowledge and denial of access to knowledge. There is also the issue of segregating secret from available information. This includes, as the hypothetical Churchill dilemma shows us, that withholding knowledge can be a tragically powerful factor. Yet it is vital, at times––to the well-being of all of us––that knowledge be channeled, sorted and evaluated.

Our personal moral life depends on how we cope with knowing too little and knowing too much. Typically, we are in ongoing situations where we have to live with a *constricted* use of knowledge. From this arise many of our dilemmas.

I have not mentioned dilemmas arising from the wonders of recent developments in biotechnology – cloning, the uses of stem cell research, and more. Here is a source of knowledge dilemmas where we have yet to identify and delineate the appropriate constrictions of the available knowledge.

I assuredly have not solved any of these knowledge dilemmas. But sometimes raising issues is worthy by itself.

Fred Emil Katz

NOTE

1   Milton Mayer, *They Thought They Were Free: The Germans, 1933-45* (Chicago: University of Chicago Press, 1971) p. 177.
2   28 ² Ibid., p. 181.

Impingings, Linkages, Shadows and the Shaping of Immediacy: Introduction

The ongoing mission of the sciences––the physical sciences, the biological sciences, as well as the human social behavior sciences–– is to discover orderliness in nature. Each science addresses that search for orderliness by carving out for itself a zone in nature where it tries to identify structures and show how they actually operate.[1]

This book operates within one zone, the search for orderliness in human social behavior. The following five essays address a particular feature within that zone. Namely, that human social behavior structures–– social institutions, social organizations, even individual careers–– often *interpenetrate* one another. The guiding premise is that the interpenetrations are, themselves, orderly. They are patterned. They are neither mystical nor haphazard. They are discernible and understandable. They are structures in their own right; they are significant.

Several forms of interpenetration will be examined, beginning with the *rider* construct. Riders are ways through which one social context can make an imprint on another, influencing its character even while the recipient context retains its separate identity. Riders can operate in a variety of ways.

1. Riders can operate "silently," adding a particular external coloration to an event while, at the same time, not permitting a fully acknowledged intrusion of that outside context. An illustration is the intrusion of a measure of sexuality into a nonsexual transaction––say, a sales transaction in a store. Precisely

because sexuality is not made overt and explicit, the rider may serve as a catalyst in the transaction; it acts as silent facilitator of the transaction. On the other hand, the sexuality rider may become explicit and come to dominate the event. Then the rider is no longer silent. The nonsexual transaction may then turn into an explicitly sexual event, or the transaction may be aborted because the intrusion of sexuality is deemed inappropriate and subversive to the integrity of the transaction.

2. Riders may remain dormant, but available for full activation at a particular time. While in a dormant state the rider may amplify and grow and become available for entirely unanticipated levels of impact. I examine this from the personal careers of some individuals, such as that of the writer Primo Levi. In his case, there was a seemingly healthy adjustment to having survived the Holocaust. Levi became a very successful writer, not only about the Holocaust but also about natural phenomena, where his zest for life was in clear view. Yet he committed suicide. Presumably, I maintain, there was a dormant rider––about the pernicious nature of survival when others did not survive, also known as survivor guilt–– that grew and grew, eventually erupting with lethal force. The growth of the dormant rider took place during the very same time as, publicly and overtly, Levi was making an apparently healthy adjustment to his survival.

3. Riders may flourish, and riders may fade. Some major historical events leave a highly impactful legacy––in the form of riders that impact the rest of our lives––whereas others, also major events, seem to leave only the most fleeting impact on our social existence. We do not know what it is in the nature of riders that might produce this difference. Why, for example, did the horrors of trench warfare in World War I leave no greater impact on subsequent generations––despite deep and profound revulsion in the earliest years after that war?

4. Riders can produce a particular kind of message, and exclude a different kind of message. An illustration is that artistic and scientific riders are apt to differ greatly. We are likely to be very moved by an exciting artistic performance, but we are given only the vaguest of commands about implementing any message. Much is left up to our own interpretation as to what the message really means. On the other hand, when we receive a medical message from our doctor, we are likely to be given precise instructions as to how this is supposed to impact our personal behavior. In the case of the artistic performance, however, the rider can give broad and emotionally charged access to our emotions and feelings. But it does not tell us what we must do as a result of the message we are receiving. By contrast, our doctor makes use of a rider that focuses our attention on specific things we must do.

Here, as in the rest of this essay, I am aware that riders are only just beginning to be understood. At this point, I am trying to open up and encourage research on rider phenomena. There is room for imaginative thinking and research to explore them further.

The essay on hidden immediacies addresses one aspect of evolution theory. After the mid-nineteenth century, when Darwin created a virtual revolution in people's awareness of evolutionary processes, a number of scholars tried to depict a form of social evolution that was based on his principles. These Social Darwinists accepted a fairly crude version of Darwinism—namely, natural selection by an environment that helped perpetuate the fittest species—and tried to apply it to human races and peoples. In the following pages I address a far more limited—and, I hope, more valid—aspect of evolution theory as applied to human beings.

Specifically, at any one point certain component parts of a system may be exempt from the prevailing struggle for survival in the present environment because they exist in a dormant state. They are not active participants in that struggle for survival being waged in the face of an environment that may be quite hostile. They can survive, perhaps even grow and prosper, because they are *not* in an active state. This is the "hidden immediacy" that can permit very divergent options—even morally poisonous ones from the point of view of the prevailing orthodoxy—to continue to be perpetuated within the social repertoire of a society. They exist in a protective cocoon.

It is possible (although I do not discuss it) that not all dormant structures are necessarily morally harmful. Some of them may produce some very advantageous moral protections.

The essay on immediacy of distance uses an American reporter's reaction to Russia of the 1990s as a way of looking at how people's current circumstances may encourage them to produce a very biased view of their past. In this case it was the current nostalgia for cheap sausages available during Joseph Stalin's regime while conveniently ignoring many of the horrors of that regime. The past is permitted to impinge onto the present, but in a very distorted form. Of course the observer brings his own perspective into play—impinging on the report—namely, his version of American democracy as applied to Russian life. The current shortage of food, although acknowledged, is not given credit for the primordial impact it is having on the hapless Russian citizens who were interviewed.

Morally speaking, are we more advanced than our "primitive" ancestors? When it comes to creating cruelties, mass murder and other forms of moral obtuseness, our recent past comes across horribly. In an absolute sense, it is not clear whether, morally, there is any progress over the course of human history.

However it is clear, if we allow ourselves to look, that we humans create moral problems for ourselves in systemic ways. It grows out of the fact that humans are moral creatures, living in morally defined communities. I shall look at two such systemic ways in the essay, "Exclusivities: Shadows We Create over Our Moral World." It examines how cultivating moral exclusiveness for our own system of morality can de-legitimize moralities other than our own, and also may foster ever-more divergent exclusivities within an existing system of orthodoxy. As to the latter, many religious communities illustrate how, over time, refinements are generated as to what constitutes true adherence to the ultimate values and, simultaneously, what constitutes forbidden practices and heresy.

The essay "Shaping Immediacy: The Particular Ways We Look at the World: The Case of Gestalt Psychology," addresses ways we think and act. From Gestalt psychologists we learned that one's environment can impinge on us to shape our thinking. From a look at four kinds of cybernetics we learn that this shaping can take on a life of its own; it can be self-organizing once a particular direction has been established by the action of a rider.

In conclusion, the various forms of interpenetration––that show up as impingings into our immediate world––are not mere accidents, spreading randomness and unpredictability into our lives. On the contrary, they can be understood as orderly processes in their own right.

Fred Emil Katz

NOTE

1 Some physicists claim to be working on a theory of everything––a successor, perhaps, to a "unified" universal theory of gravitation that tantalized but eluded Einstein. Nowadays, too, astronomers claim to be on the track of theory of the creation of the universe. Let us not be intimidated by the scope and very real successes of astronomy and general physics. There is still room for creative work in other sciences.

The World of Riders--And the Dynamics of Immediacy

I. Rider Dynamics and the Workings of Immediacy

A. The case of a silent rider: It can serve as catalyst without being made fully explicit. Indeed, it is precisely because it is not made explicit that it can function as an effective catalyst.

I first wrote about riders in relation to what happens when, in an imaginary situation, a male salesperson in a shoe store sells a pair of shoes to a woman.[1] I suggested that even though the transaction is about shoes, there can nonetheless be a silent rider of sexuality that hovers over the transaction. The woman may interpret the man's statements--"these shoes look really good on you"--as statements that underwrite her sexual attractiveness to a man. The salesman may, in turn, deliberately make use of sexual allusions to persuade the woman to buy the shoes. The sex rider is usually silent; it is not explicitly put into words. But it does intrude into the transaction. It may thereby serve as a catalyst. As such, it can facilitate the transaction without being actively transformed by it.

Conceivably, however, the transaction between the woman and the salesman might become a prelude to a sexual relationship, be it protracted or ever so brief. In this case the rider has stopped being a silent catalyst. Instead, that external reality enters fully, becoming the dominant element in a new emergent interaction. I shall discuss this further in a moment.

But first, let me raise some as-yet-unanswered questions: Are there ways of predicting when a silent rider becomes a loud rider? Under which circumstances does the silent rider come out into the open?

B. The case of the not-so-silent rider: The silent rider becomes loud and explicit. It thereby dominates the immediacy.

Here is a variation of the shoe sales transaction. Recall that in the first version of the above situation sex is the rider that serves as a catalyst but is, itself, never made the explicit focus of attention in the transaction. By contrast, a variation occurs now in the imaginary interaction between the shoe salesman and the woman customer. This time sex is a rider that becomes quite explicit and quickly transforms an apparently nonsexual interaction between these two individuals into a sexual fling between them. They have only just met and, after some brief flirtation, have a sex fling. Let us assume that this is happening even though each is currently in a long-term marriage or other long-term sexual relationship.

To the two individuals the sex fling seems to make sex feel entirely different than it does with their long-term partners. Sex seems fresh and vibrantly alive, whereas with the long-term partner it seemed to have lost its vibrancy and joy.

For each of the two, sex with the old partner bore the weight of years of frustrating, disappointing life experiences. All these impinged as a *disabling rider* onto the sexual activities with the long-term partner. It made sex a painful reminder that they had hurt and failed one another in many ways. That rider pervaded their sex life to the point of making it desultory and joyless. It also affected their sense of personal worth and dignity in realms quite apart from sex. In short, the litany of bad experiences impinged not only on their sexual intimacy. It also became a rider to the rest of their shared life. It became a persistent ogre––though rarely mentioned aloud–– that haunted all else in their life.

For the two newly meeting individuals it seems that none of these impediments to sex and to a joy-filled life are present in their sexual fling with the stranger. Here an entirely new rider, comprised of ever-so briefly realized fantasy of what sex could be – leads to a moment of real joy. It seems to these partners that they have shed the disabling rider, the one that made sex so unsatisfying, graceless, or stifling with the old partner. Alas, with their long-term partners there could be a severe damper on sexual activity.

I'll concentrate on the woman. (Remember, I am describing an imaginary story) It is based on the sexual fling with the stranger forming a new rider for her behavior toward her husband. It could manifest itself in two very different ways. She might, from a feeling of guilt, suddenly be far more aggressively sexual toward her husband – much to his pleasant surprise. Or, on the other hand, she might want to end sexual relationship with him – 'I am no longer going to make compromises – whatever did I see in him?'

To summarize, for the woman's long term situation, sex was the magnet that drew into itself memory of many unhappy and unsatisfying events in her life with her husband. Now, in sex with the stranger, sex is the magnet that momentarily draws into itself the glorious *fantasy* of what her sex life could be. It is free of the dissatisfactions and bad memories associated with the old partner. It is free, also, of any reality testing. She tells herself she would never see the salesman again. Or, if she did, she would never introduce him to her friends.

The physical sex act, itself, may not be very different with the old and the new partner. Certainly the physiology of sex is not very different. But its meaning may be entirely different. There is its essence. We humans live a life of meanings. We live and die for meanings. But "meanings" do not arrive out of thin air. As the above examples illustrate, meanings are often created by a linkage of our present context and things from another context, even if that other context is largely imaginary.

In the above section I have focused on sexual activity. This is merely an illustration of how rider processes work in the confines of one valued sphere of life. I could have illustrated the same processes from other spheres, such as eating, drinking, fighting wars, career activities, religiosity, making money, or family-focused living, to mention just a few. In the matter of eating, for example, the focus would not be the physiology of eating but the socially institutionalized format of eating, the culture of eating. The proverbial mother's chicken soup as a remedy for all illness is a symbolic summary of food's linkage to a nurturing and controlling mother and her bonding with her child. In time of sickness, this bonding is reiterated and emphasized. Through the donation of chicken soup the sick person is told that one is not alone. A loved one is coming to the rescue. She – your mother – arrives as a life-giver, a life sustainer. She will take care of you. Here is a supreme rider of nurturance.

Recall and compare the British variant of meeting many a crisis with the initial response: Let us sit down and have a cup of tea. If nothing else, this surely provides a momentary breathing space against overly hasty responses to a crisis. It can create a linkage to the life of reason, to the culture of deliberation and balanced weighing of issues, to potentials for friendship——all activated amid a crisis that may just have erupted over conflicting interests between individuals who are now facing each other.

The intrusion into tea drinking of an elaborate decorum of mannered behavior—pouring the tea from a pot, assuring just the right temperature of the tea, adding the appropriate amount of milk—further links the tea ceremony to other zones of "civilized" communal living. Here we have riders of mannered behavior that link tea drinking to other areas of life, reminding the participants in no uncertain terms that a wider social reality is relevant and bearing down on their immediate, present concerns. Here having tea becomes an occasion in which external riders give a distinctive character and meaning to a sociable interaction and, in turn, this precisely orchestrated interaction can be the source of a distinctive rider to other spheres of life in which the participating actors are engaged. The tea-drinking ceremony may, for instance, have induced some civility into these other spheres.

What I have just said about riders could be applied to the culture of drinking, as in a pub in Ireland. Here the sociability of drinking opens up to almost every sector of one's daily life. One might laugh and cry about them. You are among friends in conviviality of drinking – so almost anything goes. Riders -- the bearers of much about one's life – reign supreme, they bring connectedness into the open amid the conviviality in the pub.

Similarly, one sees the connectedness supplied by riders in the ways wars are fought and occasionally venerated and justified; the ways career activity is colored by its social linkages – my son the doctor; the ways religious activity, such as one's affiliations and participation in formal religions, is linked to nonreligious spheres of one's life – where weddings, a civilian bonding, is typically done as a religious ceremony; how such aspirations as making money can be suffused by non-economic attachments and concerns – where wealth is regarded as worldly success and moral worth.

In each of these, any specific activity in our life is suffused with riders that give it meaning through linkage to specific external spheres. They do so by attaching that specific activity to certain external spheres. In turn, the specific activity, such as sexual activity, eating, drinking, making war, or performing religious ritual, can become riders to the other spheres of our life. As to the latter, the specific character of an activity—be it joyful or desultory sex, haphazard or ceremonial eating—can become riders to the other spheres of our life, thereby giving a particular coloration to them. For instance, the joyful sex with the new partner in the first example is apt to have disastrous consequences for the relationship between the participants and their long-term spouses. It will take the form of new riders making an imprint on the long-term spousal relationship. Notably, sexual intercourse with the old partner may now seem entirely unacceptable and "destructive" to what one wants from life, most especially the newly discovered sense of freedom and joy through sex.

In short, any of the spheres of living––such as the sphere of sexual activity––can be a crucial shunting station for our life's meaning. Here, a particular set of meanings is going to crystallize, based on a particular set of confluent riders. In turn, this shunting station can serve as a reservoir of meanings that may attach to the other spheres of our life.

In another book I discussed a rider process in regard to a very large shunting station, (although I did not use that term), namely, the situation in Hitler's Germany.[2] Hitler deliberately created a rider from the myth of Germany's shame for having been defeated in World War I and having been "unjustly" punished by the victorious nations. He used the rider to permeate German thought so thoroughly, fostering such national rage, that it granted him the freedom to engage in horrendous deeds in the name of washing away Germany's shame. The rider colored much of the immediacy of life in Germany during the Nazi era. It consisted of a particular myth, creating a particular mindset, that enlisted many Germans in unlimited ferocity.

Immediacy may be entirely dominated by a rider's external message. A new rider may produce the mandate for exercising a new vitality in an individual's life, as in the sexual illustration. It may also provide a mandate for horrendous actions on a large scale, as in Nazi Germany. In each case, the participating individuals believe they are the bearers of a reality that is distinctive and unique––so much so that it may be worth abandoning a spouse or supporting a lunatic political quest. In each case there is a rider that serves as a vital catalyst to new "meaning" individuals see for their lives. It may become very explicit, resulting in changed behavior in the immediacy where people's lives are lived.

Finally, I return to the first part of this essay: Let us not assume that only loudly proclaimed riders have an impact on human actions. Silent riders, too, can have great impact. I am reminded of Indira Gandhi's first visit to the United States and the Soviet Union after she became India's prime minister. She came to request badly needed economic aid for her country. No one could accuse Mrs. Gandhi of sexually flirting with the leaders of these countries. But her manner was so charming, so sexually tinged, that President Lyndon Johnson proclaimed that he would give her anything she wanted. The usually dour Aleksey Kosygin, the Soviet premier, was temporarily transformed into an animated, gracious host. Both Johnson and Kosygin produced generous aid for India.

II. The Case of Dormancy and Malignancy——Riders That Grow While They Exist in a Silent Format[3]

A disturbing fact of life is that riders that are dormant are not necessarily stable. They may grow, even though they are not visible. Although dormant, they may become dangerous potentials for malignancy. Yet they may actually be malignant only when activated. When they are activated they may be unexpectedly lethal. (Perhaps there is a parallel to cancer in the human body. Perhaps aberrations in the DNA are dangerous only when they are activated. If so, then the secret lies in the mechanisms of activation.)

Two well-known Holocaust survivors come to mind: Primo Levi and Jerzy Kosinski.[4] Each became a distinguished writer after his own Holocaust experiences. It seemed that each had found a way to live an effective and productive life after surviving the Holocaust. Rather than wallowing in impotent depression, they found ways to be creative. Instead of continually harping on the horrors they had known, they wrote insightfully and rewardingly about life's promises and joys (while also writing insightfully about the horrors). Yet each of them eventually committed suicide. Despite their apparent success at surmounting survivor guilt, they ended their lives by their own hands.

Did they, and several other survivors who became successful writers who committed suicide (In the case of Primo Levi, there lingers some doubt whether his death was a suicide.), believe they did not deserve to live? More important for the issue I am discussing, was the sense of personal guilt never entirely obliterated from their personal psyche, and, instead, did it remain a dormant element in their makeup? If so, it seems that we must realize that the "dormant" item may actually continue to grow——like an undiscovered tumor before it eventually becomes known because it invades a vital organ. Apparently the dormant item can continue to grow even when it is not visible, and sometimes emerges suddenly, with lethal force.

The issue is not confined to Jews or to Holocaust survivors. Clarence Page, an African-American journalist, wrote about his first wife, also an African-American journalist.[5] She was born in appalling urban ghetto circumstances. Through sheer determination, discipline and effort she succeeded in leaving the ghetto and becoming a distinguished journalist, with many awards and much public acclaim coming her way. Yet she continued to feel torn by conflict––toward the white world and, also, toward the world of African-Americans where, she felt, a "successful" person simply did not fit. She committed suicide.

It seems that here, too, the dormant sense of guilt became increasingly potent even as its bearer became more "successful" in apparently overcoming obstacles to living an effective and rewarding life. It culminated, finally, in this dormant cancer becoming fully activated in a virulent, life-denying form. It seems that while this woman grew to become more and more successful, guilt about succeeding, too, kept on growing, albeit in dormant form until it finally erupted with lethal force, just as it may have done for Primo Levi and Jerzy Kosinski. (I have picked just three cases. Many more exist. Marilyn Monroe comes to mind––whose public adoration did not keep her from eventually taking an overdose of sleeping pills. Another sex goddess, Marlene Dietrich, had a real-life sexuality that became increasingly remote from the taunting sexuality for which she was celebrated. She did not commit suicide.)

Is there a process whereby an occasional monster within us is being fed even as its obverse twin––the successful, life-affirming individual––appears to win? Was Lea Page under greater pressure than the pre-civil rights movement Uncle Tom who smilingly accepted humiliation? She surely operated under a different rider, one that stated that second-class citizenship was not acceptable. Did she then, by the minute, recognize, respond to, and place in storage––not in deep storage, but in readily accessible storage–– every single racial humiliation that persisted and came her way? She presumably kept account in a very different way than any Uncle Tom. In her life a different sort of rider was at work, one that included a *multiplier effect* to each humiliation––whereas in Uncle Tom the rider included a *dissipating effect* that enabled him to accept humiliation without loss of dignity; this was often made possible by riders from a strong religious community. In Lea Page's system of accounting, anger and despair grew until eventually it burst out into the open, exacting its final cruel price.

In the cases I have mentioned a sense of guilt is shorthand for domination by a rider that connects the individual's ongoing life to an impossible world; it creates an impossible immediacy, where life can become untenable. In psychology there is an entire research literature on cognitive dissonance that touches on this reality. Here the individual is faced with untenable alternatives. Usually, one finds ways of juggling the alternatives so that the individual can, somehow, continue to function.

By contrast, it seems to me that when one element of the individual's psychological life is dormant––silent, but continuing to grow––the degree of dissonance can grow to unlivable and untenable dimensions. The dormant element is rarely subject to reality testing and control, even while it continues to silently grow and grow, as an obverse twin parasitically lodged within the outwardly successful individual. When it does finally erupt into the open it can do so with life-destroying consequences.

That "obverse twin," so thoroughly different from the public and openly known individual, can also contain real evil, even among individuals who are unusually good in their public behavior. Psychiatrist M. Scott Peck has studied this intensively.[6] He reports an analysis of two persons who were evidently "possessed" by evil. Within them there coexisted not merely goodness, but the potential for holiness; "the core personality of each seemed unusually good and potentially saintly."[7] In the ongoing life of an individual, does the cultivation of holiness––of goodness in the most profound way–– simultaneously open up storage, in dormant form, of its opposite? Concerning the two persons Peck studied, he states: "Indeed, I have reason to suspect that the potential holiness of these two people was one of the reasons for their possession [by evil]."[8]

Within a given individual is such creation of evil the inevitable antithesis to goodness, or is this merely a possibility? Am I fantasizing altogether? Peck, whose thesis is that evil is largely caused by narcissism–– namely, excessive self-love––would probably answer these questions by saying that the individual who has commitment to something greater than oneself––such as God, truth or love––gains such transcending freedom that evil has no place in one's makeup.

III. Rider Flourishing, Rider Fading

Why are some rider imprints so short-lived? (And why are some so long-lived?) Does not the very intensity of the initial imprint guarantee some longevity of impact? At this point, I have no answers. Only disturbing questions.

America entered World War II immediately after Japanese forces attacked the American naval port of Pearl Harbor. That event had a momentous impact. Here was an event that seemed to create a fundamentally transforming imprint on the American psyche. Americans suddenly found out that modern warfare could intrude into their own territory and do so with lethal impact. America was not immune to the horrors of "distant" wars; America was vulnerable.

The attack on Pearl Harbor became a rider to the nation's outlook. It focused the country's energy on marshaling resources to fight the external enemy. It seemed to change, perhaps permanently, an entire generation's outlook about America.

Yet, fifty years later, who now mentions "Pearl Harbor"? If one does mention it, it no longer resonates with the same searing impact it once had. "Pearl Harbor" has faded. Who would have thought that Americans would ever forget "Pearl Harbor?"

In an earlier section I discussed persisting, long-lasting riders. Here, however, I have just indicated another attribute of riders: Sometimes riders flourish, with seemingly overwhelming and unstoppable impact, only to fade away into thin air, leaving barely a residue of their once-powerful force. Perhaps nowhere is this more striking than in the ephemeral impact of the horrors of warfare. At one point in time we are struck by the horrors of warfare. We are torn asunder by the emotional impact of what we hear and, since the advent of television, what we see up close. Then we forget about it.

It is altogether amazing that the horrors of war have not intruded more urgently and more decisively––and more lastingly––into our consciousness and into the social arrangements whereby we lead our lives. After the end of World War I, for example, it was thought that the horrors of trench warfare—with their huge number of killings in the form of direct, hand-to-hand combat, where virtually an entire generation of men of several countries massacred one another— would lead to such revulsion that it would put an end to mass warfare. To be sure there was momentary revulsion. There was, for example, poignant literature—such as *All Quiet on the Western Front*—that portrayed the boundless horrors. It did not, however, produce a permanent stop to such horrors. There were moving films that portrayed the horrors. There were innumerable eyewitness and survivor reports of the horrors. They, too, did not result in an ending of the horrors of warfare.

Stated more technically, warfare did not result in a flourishing of riders from these events that would make such an imprint of these horrors on the surviving people's lives that further events of this nature simply could not happen again. Here I am not talking merely about moral outrage and shock but about an imprint on the existing social structures of societies, so that as a result there would be created a social order that ruled out participation in warfare.

There was some flourishing of horror riders. These resulted in efforts to create an international order—such as the League of Nations after World War I—that would see to it that conflicts between nations would be handled peacefully. But the League of Nations failed. (It failed for many reasons. One of these, surely, was that its principal sponsor, the American president, could not get his own Congress to support it.) Further wars did take place. The horrors of World War I did not leave any noticeable imprint in the form of riders that would totally rule out war. The horror riders faded.

I must reiterate: In this section I offer no firm answers, only disturbing questions that demonstrate a woeful state of our moral existence and, also, great deficiency in our science of riders. We know that riders may flourish and riders may fade. We do not know, at this time, whether these occur in patterned ways. Perhaps we shall eventually discover regularities and rules, even laws that govern these patterns of rider flourishing and fading. (I shall continue this exhortation at the end of this essay.)

IV. Connectivity and Immediacy: Riders That Link

Who, while listening to the ending of Giacomo Puccini's *La Boheme* would not be prepared to give one's own life if only Mimi could live? Exists there so cold a person who would not gladly make this sacrifice or at least fantasize doing so? Who, on experiencing an outstanding performance of this opera, does not feel connected to the experience? Not only feeling connected but entwined, intimately and personally, with something very transcendent, profound, all triggered by seeing and hearing this artistic masterpiece.

Entwined with what? The answer will differ for each of us. To one person, it is with the sweetness of love; to another it is to life's vulnerability; to yet another it is to selflessness; to fate; to nirvana and unblemished bliss. Many more vital reference points could be listed. Each of us will find a version of entwining, depending on what we individually hold most dear and vulnerable.

The actual plot of *La Boheme* could scarcely be less earthshaking. It gives a snapshot of the struggling lives of young artists––their poverty, petty quarrels, efforts to do creative work amid a world of hardship and annoyances, such as landlords who insist on being paid the rent. What transforms this potentially dreary scene into a shatteringly powerful experience is the artistry that is being brought to bear––how the story is told and, most of all, the music and its performance.

This combination of a story with unexcelled artistry creates a linkage for the audience. That linkage connects us to some of the most profoundly personal features we envision for our own lives. The performance is the catalyst that becomes, briefly, a rider to our own life. That rider brings us close––it connects us––to some of our own purest yearnings and aspirations. As a rider, it suffuses our lives, however briefly, with a sense of access to something profound. Of course, what that profundity consists of differs for each one of us. What counts is that we feel that we are given access to it, at least for a moment.

However, an artistic performance gives us a message––the access to something profoundly important to ourselves––in a very privileged way. We can "experience" the sense of access to this message without having to do anything about it. After we leave the theater we are under no obligation to live up to the briefly awakened sensibility of what is most important to us. We can leave it all behind after we have applauded.[9] On the other hand, the awakening may indeed have a lasting impact on how we henceforth lead our lives. But the performance itself cannot ensure that we will do so.

The form of the artistically delivered message is characteristically undefined. It is up to us, individually, to clarify the message for ourselves. This has the great advantage that we can, and must, tailor the message to our own needs, concerns and capabilities of understanding. There is virtually no limit to the variety of messages we can derive. Puccini has no control whatsoever over what message you derive from his masterpiece. This goes for all artists, once their work is handed over to the public domain.

The negative side of this is that any implementation of a message, even any clarification of what the message means, is left entirely up to the vagaries of personal whim. There are no directives as to what to do after receiving an artistic message. There is no moral obligation to transform one's life on the basis of the message. How many people have purified their lives after hearing *La Boheme?* In all likelihood, only the tiniest fraction of even those who were deeply moved by it have done so.

Stated differently, the *La Boheme* rider gives a very short-lived transformation to the listener. It usually leaves little, if any residue. There is no moral imperative to incorporate the new access to one's profoundest yearnings and convictions into one's actions tomorrow and thereafter.

By contrast, when you receive a "scientific" message from your doctor—that you had better make some changes in your eating habits because of a linkage to your current health—you are under a "moral obligation" to implement this message. Here the rider is very different. It impinges onto your life in a far more direct and decisive way. It is far more focused and authoritative than the artistic rider. It gives you few choices—much fewer than the artistic message. It gives a very different coloration to immediacy. It demands— morally—that the link to your health requires action.

By contrast, the *La Boheme* link to your immediate world, so much more powerful and transcendent in its vision, contains no moral imperative that its profound vision is anything more than a brief mirage that you have admired because it has shaken you beautifully and profoundly. You will surely see *La Boheme* again. It will again move you. But you will again consider yourself entertained rather than instructed. You will again do nothing to implement its message.

V. The Holocaust and Our Own Immediacy: Rider Emanations and Rider Dissipations

Who remembers the deliberate starvation to death of some 13 million of Kulaks? Who thought we would forget the attack on Pearl Harbor?

One singular historical event produces emanations that permeate the historical landscape for ages, leaving a decisive imprint on much subsequent life in the form of riders that pervade ongoing activities. Another historical event, perhaps equally singular, leaves only the vaguest of imprints on subsequent life. As far as we know, there is little balance between the profundity of an event and its afterlife as riders to subsequent events; a fairly trivial event may enjoy a rich rider afterlife, whereas a powerful event may die utterly and entirely, leaving no trace. What is more, emanations from singular events can produce highly unpredictable riders. Yet––for good or ill––their impact may be real and profound.

An eminent philosopher says about the Holocaust, "Humanity has lost its claim to continue . . . we are all stained by it." For Christians, he says, "the Holocaust has shut the door that Christ opened . . . nullifying the redemption out of humanity's fallen state" given through Christ; "the Christian era has closed." "The human species is now de-sanctified; if it were ended or obliterated now, its end would no longer constitute a special tragedy." "The Holocaust is a massive cataclysm that distorts everything around it."[10]

He reminds us that in the Holocaust humankind enacted a level of evil––of cruelty, murder, and assault on human dignity––that surpassed all others in known human experience. This event, the philosopher tells us, has stained us all. It had and still has a singular impact on all human endeavors.

In terms of the orientation I am developing here, one can rephrase the philosopher's statement, claiming that the Holocaust is a rider that has fundamentally transformed human existence. That rider lies as a heavy burden on our very existence as a species. It has changed it. We are being told that nothing whatsoever in the life of our species can escape its impact. (I am reporting the philosopher's statement. I am not at all sure that, in the long run, it will prove to be true. Nonetheless, it is an insightful proposition.)

The philosopher—the late Robert Nozick, of Harvard University—tries to suggest some ways to escape the horrifying curse placed on our species, such as being more empathetic to suffering wherever it takes place. But it is clear—surely even to Nozick himself—that this answer is not very persuasive. The curse remains.

Nozick speaks in moral tones. He tells us that through the one phenomenon, the Holocaust, our species lost sanctity. How many such shocks can a species absorb and still survive? He seems to think that through the Holocaust we have entirely lost our moral moorings and it would therefore be no great catastrophe if our species would end its existence. If through some natural disaster, or an accidentally triggered (or even deliberately triggered) nuclear or biochemical war we were to annihilate our entire species, it would of course be a horrifying ordeal to those of us who were here at the time of that conflagration. But morally speaking, it would be no great loss as we have already given up our moral right to exist. Morally speaking, we have made a terrible mess of our existence. As the aftermath to the Holocaust, Nozick implies, there pervades a foul rider in our moral existence.

What this philosopher drives home in eloquent moral terms must be clarified in terms of rider processes. Specifically, despite the philosopher's powerful statement about the need for a moral response, it is not at all clear whether the Holocaust has thus far produced an appropriate imprint on the existence of our species. Morally speaking, the message is loud and clear; morally, we are befouled. But it may well be that our response to the befouling is crippled. Is the answer to the Holocaust's reality loud and clear—and lasting? If so, is it translated into appropriate riders that make a discernible and viable imprint on actual social institutions, social programs and individual behaviors? In the short term, one can indeed find riders imprinting on life in the post-Holocaust world in a way that is morally responsive to the Holocaust. But what of the future, the long-term existence of our species?

To be sure Holocaust survivors, their kinfolk and a multitude of other sensitive souls have placed the Holocaust on the forefront of contemporary attention, at least in the West—after an initial period of relative inaction and silence. But the nature of this imprint——this rider——includes some anachronistic visions of life that will not ensure moral growth. Specifically, we have such notions as, "we must not forget the Holocaust, so that it will not happen again"——as though such memory would constitute a vaccine against future horrors, as though moral revulsion will oblige people to behave with moral purity in the future. Much historical experience points in the opposite direction. People can remember previous horrors and still behave horribly themselves. Indeed the horrors in the Balkans in the early 1990s were being justified by some perpetrators as retribution for horrors previously perpetrated——during the Nazi era——by the ancestors of their victims. They remembered the Holocaust.

To be sure, also, one can discern an imprint of the Holocaust on the political systems in the actions of the nations of the West. Most notably, the support for the creation of the state of Israel is a direct result of the imprint of the Holocaust on the political realm. In the economic realm, the reparations paid by German governments to Jewish Holocaust survivors, especially those living in Israel, is another result of the imprint of the Holocaust. Finally, there is the imprint on religions. Through the actions of two popes——John Paul II and John XXIII——the Catholic Church has made fundamental overtures to the Jews and Judaism that would have been unthinkable without the imprint of the Holocaust. Within the Jewish religion, the Holocaust's imprint is most pronounced of all. It has placed itself in a central position in Jewish religiosity——on a par with such events as the destruction of the temple——as a major modern rallying point and as a core focus of the sense of identity of many individual Jews.

The Holocaust as rider to the present I have just alluded to so very briefly is real and impactful. My allusions have surely not done justice to the true range and intensity of that impact. I am not going into further detail because there is real danger in assuming that the impact is powerful enough to rectify what the Holocaust has exposed so brutally and bluntly.

Has the moral dimension of the disaster, indicated by Nozick, been transformed into appropriate riders that will bring about the necessary social transformations and prophylactic measures that will ensure us against repetitions in the future? Or, as happened following other major horrors in the past, do we have fleeting emanations of anguish and abhorrence followed by dissipation of the moral ardor, without adequate genesis of riders that make a decisive imprint on our existing communal life? If history is any guide, it does not look hopeful.

Let us stand back and look at the rider emanations from other major horrors.

After World War I, it was thought that these horrors would leave such an imprint on the population and governments of the world that it would lead to a new, peaceful world where war would be outlawed. It has not. The imprint, the rider, was vague and imperfect. Yes, there were riders of revulsion of war, resulting in the attempt to create a viable League of Nations. But there were also riders of memory that left an imprint of lingering grudge on the thinking of Germans, which––exploited by Hitler––created a readiness to engage in even more horrors.

The most typical response to social horrors is that of no response, only silence. Silence greeted the purges in the Soviet Union under Stalin. Silence greeted the surviving Armenians after the massacres by Turks. Silence greeted the murders in China during the Cultural Revolution. And so it goes. Individually, each of these horrors is smaller in scale than the Holocaust. But cumulatively, they surpass it manifold. We are talking of killings, in the twentieth century alone, in the range of well over one hundred million people.

Moral outrage is, sad to say, rather cheap. It is often impotent in confronting the practical realities of our social existence. One cannot assume that social horrors––such as mass killings––will produce riders of moral aversion that will, then, turn into vaccines against horrors in the form of imprints on future behavior.

The entire thesis about riders rests on the assumption that there can be an imprint of one event on others that may be widely separated from it in time and space. The imprint is based on an emanation from one event, which then intrudes into another event in the form of a rider. Morally speaking, this can work for good or ill. There can be entirely wicked riders, just as there can be highly laudable riders. Dispassionately speaking, there can be some riders that energize, that spur action by its host, whereas others may generate inhibition and passivity––such as Woodrow Wilson's effort to create a world peace-saving League of Nations rejected by the American Congress, which operated under a different set of riders than he did.

Usually verbal symbols are the vehicles that transmit the message from the emanating situation to the recipient situation, bringing with it riders that impinge onto that new situation. The very mention of such terms as Pearl Harbor, the War of Independence, the Civil War, the Alamo, the French Revolution, the Vietnam War, slavery, the Great Depression, and, of course, the Holocaust will at once trigger some realization that these events have produced a moral emanation that is still with us.

What is not at all clear is precisely what sort of riders are being "carried" by these verbal messages. How is the message transformed into palpable imprints on ongoing behavior? Or is the message dissipated into empty posturing? Speaking of emanations being dissipated, under which circumstances do riders not take root? What constitutes rider "fertility," resulting in successful impregnation of a new social soil with the message from the emanating source?

Speaking of dissipations, retired General George Lee Butler and sixty other generals and admirals from around the world "issued a call for rapid nuclear disarmament . . . [saying] he had learned in his former position as commander of U.S. nuclear forces how easy it might be for a simple mistake to start a nuclear war."[11] The author of that article goes on to state: "His intervention, together with that of his fellow officers, will reverberate for years to come."[12] I wish I could believe that. If previous revulsions against war are any guide, this new warning––by those most qualified to issue it––will dissipate into thin air. Their words will not take root in the soil of our current world. What would it take to make sure that their words would become riders that generate appropriate action? This is a reason why we must undertake the basic work of understanding, as dispassionately as possible, how riders work. Yes, the possibility of nuclear annihilation is terribly real and terribly important. But even more important is that we get more effective grasp of how riders work––how even the threat of nuclear annihilation might simply be ignored because it fails to become an effective rider to our ongoing social activities.

Returning to verbal messages, we must realize that the words that act as conveyers of specific meaningful messages, in the form of riders, are ones that are being activated in the recipient situation––and refer back to the supposed emanating situation rather than the other way around, of the emanating situation automatically triggering specific meaningful messages. Hence, the clues as to which riders will find a hospitable home depends very heavily on the recipient situation—its readiness to receive a particular message and, then, to act on the message it has received.

Although I have devoted a number of pages to the nature of riders, it is surely clear that we still have much to learn about them. Are there "laws" that govern rider processes, waiting to be discovered, so that we might then gain some mastery over emanations that are transformed into riders which intrude into other events? Why do some events trigger loud emanations that become riders urgently yet briefly impinginng on us – the early cry "Remember Pearl Harbor"—while others trigger only repression and silence? What about the process of selecting the content of riders? What sort of selectivity was at work when, for example, Germans of the 1920s were left with a sense of grudge as the major imprint from the 1914-1918 war onto their daily life, rather than a sense of total abhorrence of war? Or, was their abhorrence of war placed in a recessive niche, being dominated by the grudge syndrome? Are there dominant and recessive riders?

I operate from the conviction that we can indeed discover regularities— laws, perhaps—in the workings of riders. But we are only just getting started. I invite the reader to join in this enterprise. We are not alone. Insightful poets and novelists have long recognized the intrusions of wider worlds into our immediate world of daily living. And so have physicists, recognizing and refining knowledge of gravitational forces that have impact at great distance, and still searching for a universal theory of gravitation that explains impingings more fully. In the language of riders, there are emanations from particular events, there are intrusions from these events into new contexts, and there are dissipations of riders altogether. As we learn how such processes work we may, at long last, find ways to create more effective imprintings against horrors.

Perhaps, then, we shall cease to *be* impotent bystanders to the repetition of mass horrors.

NOTE

1   Fred Emil Katz, "Social Structure and Social Participation," *Social Forces* (1966): 199-200.

2   Fred Emil Katz, *Ordinary People and Extraordinary Evil* (Albany, NY: 1993), for example, pp. 37-40.

3   The chapter on escalating dualities picks up some of the same issues raised in the present chapter.

4   I shall discuss these two men's lives again at greater length in the section on career dualities.

5   Clarence Page, "Survivor guilt: the angst of the black bourgeoisie," *The Sun* (Baltimore), March 11, 1996.

6   See M. Scott Peck, *People of the Lie: The Hope for Healing Human Evil* (New York: Simon and Schuster, Touchstone Books, 1983); also John A. Sanford, *Evil: The Shadow Side of Reality* (Crossroads: 1981); Malachi Martin, *Hostage to the Devil (New York*: Bantam Books, 1977).

7   Peck, *People of the Lie*, p. 194.

8   Ibid.

9   Fred Emil Katz, "A Third Culture," *Studies in Sociology* (Milton Albrecht, ed., State University of New York, Buffalo, NY: 1967). What I am calling the "third culture" is the interstitial domain between theoretically knowing something and applying that knowledge.

10 Robert Nozick, *The Examined Life* (New York: Simon and Schuster, 1988), pp. 238-241.

11 Jonathan Power, "The taming of the warrior class," *The Baltimore Sun,* December 13, 1996.

12 Ibid.

Impingings of Dormant and Hidden Immediacies

Ralph Gerard, a neurophysiologist, declared that evolution is the "production of novelty by the organism and its fixing by the environments."[1] As seen by Darwin natural selection is brought about chiefly by the action of the environment, where "organisms are passively chosen or rejected." Lamarck, by contrast, "emphasized the organism as the major variable; organisms actively achieve their adaptation." In actuality, said Gerard, "Both factors, of course, operate."

The challenge is to discover just how organisms and their environments do, in fact, come to terms. How, over time, do they accommodate each other? What adaptive capacities are at work? These are very broad issues. In the following essay I shall discuss one particular adaptive capacity, to clarify how it operates and see what advantages it confers in the struggle for survival in an environment.

My query is: Does dormancy of a component part of a system––of a structural component, of a behavior pattern or even of a specific set of beliefs––provide a unique adaptive capacity for survival in the Darwinian sense?

Here the "dormant" item is not subject to the ongoing, active vicissitudes that influence survival in an environment. It can persist (survive) even when it would have been killed off by the environmental circumstances if it had been in an "active" state. For example, prejudices (such as anti-Semitism or racism) are sometimes believed to be eliminated through public education that addresses these prejudices. Yet if the prejudices are dormant they may not be reachable through efforts to educate. The prejudices may exist in dormant form within a cocoon that makes them impervious to the educational efforts of the "active" components of the society. Hence there may be a hidden sector that makes the active societal playing field––especially the ongoing environmental impact on the content of the society––distinctly unrealistic because it contains a subterranean content that is not being reached.

Perhaps the subterranean structures are just a variant of a very common attribute of all structures that have a stable interaction with an environment (including, even, any social system that interacts with a social environment). Namely, that many structures operate from within a protective cocoon——where only some aspects are subject to the vicissitudes of the environment, and other aspects are not; where the environment is restricted from having total impact on a structure.

For example, Gerard notes, the nervous system is in many ways protected. "This organ is wrapped in multiple membranes, floated in liquid . . . encased in bony armor——all giving maximal protection against mechanical damage. Carotid receptors help insure a constant supply of blood of proper composition at the portal of the brain, and the state of the bathing fluid is further under precise regulation from central receptors for osmotic pressure, temperature, carbon dioxide, et cetera, which supplement the peripheral regulators . . . [and many more] The nervous system is indeed a well-buffered black box, protected from all input save those external and internal for which it is specifically coded."[2]

The last point is crucial. The nervous system is structured so that the environment has only certain forms of access to it. I suspect that this holds true for many structures that have, over evolutionary time, developed a stable form of existence within a particular environment. It amounts to the organism having attained a measure of control over its environment, namely, controlling the access of the environment to that organism. All this provides some degree of "hiding" for the organism's structures——in this case, the nervous system, making them able to function flexibly, free of some external control; their structured protections make it possible for a structure, such as the nervous system, to have a measure of functional autonomy. But this autonomy exists only within a specific zone——namely, the sphere which the protective cocoon in fact protects. The autonomy is not unlimited. It is "structured" within the existing system.

In terms of a calculus of autonomy, one can say that the nervous system has attained a degree of autonomy over certain parts of its environment in exchange for operating only within a limited zone of autonomy; it has attained some specified external autonomy in exchange for giving up some internal autonomy. But the retained internal autonomy includes the capacity to remain free of external supervision and control in certain sectors of activity. This compromise, reached over eons of evolutionary time, is the "hidden immediacy" of the present.

How does functional autonomy apply to social structures? For example:

1. The traditional Western family has many ways in which it is protected from its surroundings––from prying by the state, the community, and neighbors––giving its members the autonomy to engage in activities that are not directly supervised by the environment. This autonomy is achieved through formal (legal) as well as informal mechanisms. In this exchange it is presumed that the family will exercise its autonomy only within certain limits. For example, the family will not use its autonomy to murder its members––if it did, all bets are off; its autonomy as a family will be dissolved. But short of such extremes, the hidden immediacy of family life is that they are accorded a great deal of autonomy in the form of privacy as to how families organize the life of their members.

2. The case of military units within American society: Traditionally, despite an overall civilian control over the military, ongoing military practices enjoy a considerable amount of protection from prying (and supervision) by the civilian sector. This makes it possible for military units to train and engage in acts of killing that would be anathema if carried out in the civilian sector. The hidden immediacy, here, is that very different moral worlds can coexist. In one, killing may be regarded as entirely abhorrent. In the other, killing may be occasionally necessary and, even, laudable. This dualism is accomplished through socially approved zones of autonomy––each operating within boundaries, yet linked to the larger social community, while at the same time operating within a moral zone of its own. From the standpoint of the larger society, the killing operations of the military units may be largely hidden. From the standpoint of the military units, certain moral standards of the larger society may, in turn, be largely hidden.

I am speaking of psychological hiding of military killings. With the advent of television coverage of military operations, which began to reach an entirely new level in the Vietnam War, the process of psychological hiding of killings by the military has become more complicated and less tenable. Yet, as the Gulf War of the 1990s indicated, military killings can still find broad approval locally and even nationally, if wrapped in other immediacies (such as wanting to use this opportunity to wash away the American military's still-burning shame about the loss of the Vietnam War).

Let me return to dormancy; namely, that some component parts of a society's cultural configuration——some culture patterns, some beliefs, customs and practices——are perpetuated in a dormant state. Perhaps here, in exchange for temporarily renouncing active participation in ongoing affairs, there can be a hiding of currently entirely unacceptable practices, such as vicious attack against a particular group that is currently socially accepted and treated with approval by the wider society; yet the unacceptable culture components are able to persist in their inactive, dormant mode. The "exchange" may be predicated on the promise of not activating them in a disruptive manner, or activating them only under certain circumstances—— just as biological organisms permit killer "antibodies" to exist within the organism, in a dormant state, on the presumption that they will be activated only when certain conditions arise.

I can only speculate as to why and how, in human societies, such dormancies of potentially hurtful elements are allowed to persist, rather than being eradicated. Perhaps, from the perspective of the larger system, it would be too costly, too disturbing, too expensive in quite a narrow sense, to obliterate the dormant items rather than letting them persist in supposedly innocuous dormant ways. It may also be too difficult to detect horrors when they exist only in a dormant mode, as mere rudiments——as mere "prejudices" against a particular category of persons——that might or might never reach a fully malignant, phenotypic concreteness.

The hidden elements may not seem to be "immediate," since they are not fully active. Hence they may be permitted, perversely, to pursue extreme options——just as political parties that are out of power may be permitted to engage in extremist politics because they are deemed to be innocuous and ineffectual. Here the hidden immediacy is that there exists a tacit agreement between the party in power and the party out of power. In exchange for not being given power, the excluded parties are permitted to cultivate a culture that includes irresponsibly esoteric behavior. They are granted a zone of autonomy that, supposedly, won't hurt the larger system. Their esoterics are seemingly shunted into dead-end sidings. Woe to tranquility, then, when those sidings prove to lead back to the main track, and the esoterics are suddenly upon us——as they were in 1994 in American politics. At that time a larger number of Representatives were elected to office from among those who had been practicing ideological slash-and-burn tactics in their former niche as outsiders. Similarly, the zealotry of the out-of-power factions that produced the French Revolution became lethal——even to those factions themselves——when the revolution succeeded in gaining power. That revolution, like some others, was notorious for devouring its own members once it gained power. It did so when the factions continued the zealotries they had nurtured before they came to power.

A crucial question remains: Just how do hidden immediacies serve as havens for and occasions of horrendous deeds? Note: The very assimilated German Jews in the twentieth century, the very assimilated conversos in Spain in the fifteenth century, and the peacefully coexisting Croats and Serbs of Bosnia in the twentieth century. In all of these benign integration seemed to have obliterated hatred among diverse groups. Yet it was precisely there——where peaceful coexistence seemed to have progressed so very far—— that the most horrific actions were suddenly activated. Here such outbreaks were least expected. How could this happen in these, of all places?

In each of the just-mentioned cases, the "active" immediacies——how the diverse groups actually lived together——seemed to have eradicated the ethnic and religious hatreds. Yet it turned out hatred (or a potential for hatred) must have persisted in dormant and hidden form. Perhaps it is precisely when there is a public reconciliation of long-standing differences that there can be retained a small but increasingly recalcitrant remnant of "differences" (ranging from hatred to minor suspicion, prejudice, or fear), which remain encapsulated, in an unreachable cocoon, in the cultural repertoire. Perhaps because these differences are no longer publicly mentionable in the currently prevailing climate of opinion, their encapsulation becomes increasingly impermeable and therefore resistant to change or eradication. Given their impermeability, the remaining sectors of hatred and suspicion can retain their esoteric content, and even nurture it——as in vitriolic anti-Semitic publications, such as *The Protocols of the Elders of Zion*——within its protected niche.

Stated differently, perhaps the unfashionable "differences"––the hatred, fear and prejudice against particular target groups––are so thoroughly repackaged that they become invisible to the larger society. They exist in a cultural cocoon that is impervious to the wider society's constraints and supervision. From that setting they can actively protect and even cultivate and foster pockets of extreme hatred and rage. What makes currently dormant pockets of rage so dangerous is that they can become available for full activation once a suitable catalyst arrives on the scene. That catalyst may come from critical incidents––such as the loss of a war, or an economic downturn––that shake the foundation of the existing peace among social factions, among political adversaries, among the haves and have-nots. It may come from rabble-rousing leaders who capitalize on this situation to gain power. It may also come from a wide range of citizens being persuaded that their own personal interests are at stake, allowing themselves to be mobilized and recruited.

In contrast to the conventional wisdom, the process of activation may be slow and drawn out over a long period of time. In the case of the converses in Spain, for example, the process of activation of dormant but fertile pockets of hatred took almost half a century, triumphing after many setbacks. Perhaps each setback left behind, in dormant storage, an increasingly viable residue of focused ill will against the conversos, available for future activation. In short, the dormant poison may have continued to grow even while it was in a dormant state. During that time of dormancy it may have undergone a process of slow feeding of its cocooned poisonous content. Each public setback served to add yet another increment of discontent to its body of yearnings.

In the case of Germany, the process of activation of unrivaled anti-Semitism––the transformation of dormant, diffuse hatred into initiation of an actual policy of focused and organized mass hatred–– took about fifteen years, from 1918 to 1933, when the Nazis came to power. If we examine a longer period of German history, it may turn out that anti-Semitism was on the rise over a much longer period.

In each case the process of activating the dormant component involved drastic rearrangement of the society's priorities and reallocation of the society's resources. Above all, the activation involved refocusing the society's moral climate, inducing a particular and new focus for the people's moral zeal. All this brought into existence a new immediacy, where a hidden immediacy became transformed into a public immediacy. No longer was the dormant component hidden. It was put into practice openly; it now became the reigning orthodoxy, against which opposition became increasingly unpopular.

I began this chapter with the query that dormancy––of a particular component part of a culture or organism––might provide a unique kind of adaptive capacity, in the Darwinian sense. The ensuing discussion has led me to realize that such dormancy might lead to survival of capacities that, when activated, can profoundly transform the existing immediacy. From a moral perspective, highly abhorrent moralities (from the point of view of the prevailing morality) may enjoy privileged sanctuary while in the dormant state. During that state this morality may continue to grow and, on activation, bring into full-blown immediacy an entirely changed morality, one that may be abhorrent from the previously prevailing perspective.

This also raises the issue of how one can ascertain when a genuinely dangerous social attribute exists in a dormant state and when, by contrast, a search for such dormant attributes constitutes unwarranted, McCarthyist paranoia? When are small deviations from a moral consensus, existing in a dormant state, potentially dangerous? When, by contrast, are they a reservoir of healthy diversity? Such issues can only be addressed if we gain more insight into the workings of hidden immediacies.

NOTE

1   Ralph Gerard, "Becoming: The Residue of Change," in *Sol Tax,* editor, *Evolution after Darwin,* vol. 2, *The Evolution of Man* (Chicago: University of Chicago Press, 1960).
2   43 Ibid., p. 258.

The Immediacy of Distance:
The Case of Cheap Sausage and the Acceptance of a Murderous Regime

"Apparently, people lived in a totalitarian society for seventy years without even noticing it."[1]

When they see it from a distance a new immediacy is created, based on quite specific linkages to that distant past. In turn, these linkages facilitate quite specific impingings of that past into the present.

An insightful and sensitive American observer traveling on the Trans-Siberian Railroad in 1995 found himself amazed that Russians were looking back on the Stalin era with nostalgia. They spoke fondly of those times, when sausages were cheap, "you could take a train to the city and buy sausage for two rubles and thirty kopeks. Not just any sausage, but Moskovskaya sausage."[2] Ah, those were the days!

It seems that they totally ignored the horrors of Stalinism––the gulags, purges, and its absence of even rudimentary freedom for the Soviet people. "After experiencing one of the most violent and repressive regimes the world has ever known, why do people bother to ask each other if they remember when sausage cost 2.30?"[3]

Brian Humphreys, the author of the report, tells us that Westerners, himself included, have a different view of totalitarianism than those who actually lived under it. The latter may see some good things––such as economic security amid their general poverty––whereas the outsider sees only harsh oppression and pain. This is particularly poignant when people's present situation––so much more free, so much richer in opportunities–– contains great unpredictability and poverty, unsoftened by governmental safeguards.

Some underlying features come to mind. Yes, Stalinism was totalitarian. It was harsh and brutal; it was murderous. Yet it was also a comprehensive socialist package of programs, wherein people were assured a roof over their head, relatively full medical care, a job (even if it was a miserable one), and access to an educational system that was fairly adequate. Freedom in the Western sense——of individuals being able to move from place to place, choosing any occupation for which they had competence, voting in unencumbered ways——was simply not part of that form of social existence.

Still, there was much variety within the Stalinist existence. Some parts, such as the sausage dimension——food that was cheap and available——had profound appeal. It has even more appeal, perhaps, in the early post-Communist Russia, when many do not have access to food, expensive or inexpensive, and whereupon, retrospectively, they invent a glorious past when there was no shortage of good food.

I learned from my study of Nazism that a totalitarian regime's package of programs tend to become amalgamated into one cohesive entity. This means that an individual who becomes attached to one of its components, say, an offer of job opportunities, may then become implicated in contributing to the entire package of programs, even to those components for which the individual has no personal commitment (and toward which he or she may even feel repugnance). The individual becomes attached at one node of the package, such as its economics of job opportunity, but then becomes entrapped in the entire package——not merely passively, as onlooker, but often as a very active contributor to programs for which that individual has very limited commitment.

In the case of Stalinism, a node of attachment to the totalitarian system's package may be stomach-centered——the availability of inexpensive food. But once attached to that package one is apt to forgive many of the system's excesses. Most especially, one is apt to forgive and forget one's own not-so-nice contributions to that system——such as collaborations with the secret police or taking advantage of the system's anti-Semitism by taking over property that belonged to Jews.

Two features emerge. The individual citizen may find some things explicitly worth accepting——worth living and dying for——in a system that also contains horrors that are personally repugnant. But, tacitly or explicitly, one has accepted the system in its entirety. Given an ongoing life where one must make compromises, one may well ignore the horrors while getting on with life. Furthermore, while living within the house of horrors that was Stalinism, one had little freedom and little incentive to acknowledge, even to oneself, just how horrible was that system and one's own contributions to making it work.

In the 1990s (when I first prepared this essay) the immediate urgencies surrounding inadequate food——and a multitude of other inadequacies that came forth at that time——become dominant riders when looking at the past. They color many Russians' perspective about that past, obscuring the horrors while ennobling and exaggerating the availability of inexpensive food. It is precisely the distance from the past that creates a new "reality" about that past. It produces a new immediacy, comprised of active disparagement of the present alongside a largely fictitious ennoblement of the past.

Viewed from the West, one can see entirely different perspectives to Stalinism. There is the view that sees his regime as the epitome of Communist cruelties and repression of freedom, coupled with military expansionism and messianic international Communism that was attempting to convert the rest of the world to the Utopian vision of Marxism, and doing so by subversion and secret intrusions into the political life of other countries.

Actually, the Western view of Stalinism has also undergone some changes. During the height of Stalinism, particularly during the post-World War II Cold War era, the Western view operated under the prevailing rider that Stalinist Communism was an active threat to the West, through efforts to subvert Western political systems. It threatened the West militarily, through its build-up of a nuclear arsenal as well as huge conventional forces. And it threatened the West ideologically, by offering a seemingly beautiful Utopian version of socialism, whose imperfections were largely hidden due to an absence of a free press and prevention of unsupervised access by outsiders to life in the Soviet Union.

Since the end of the Cold War the Western view of Stalinism has become more focused on the internal horrors of Soviet society at the time, its stark differences from Western notions of personal freedom and political participation by the citizenry, and the lack of an infrastructure conducive to capitalism as it is practiced in the West, especially in the United States.

In short, the West's prevailing rider, as the Post-Cold War West confronts the former Stalinism, derives from the viewpoint that democratic capitalism is an appropriate secular religion, one that all nations ought to follow. This capitalism requires certain realms of freedom and certain ways of participation by the citizenry——many of which were throttled by Stalinism. In this perspective the positive sides of life under Stalinism are entirely ignored. For example, under Stalin's rule, the Soviet citizen was accustomed to being told where to live. Yet that same citizen was also accustomed to assuming that the state would provide a place to live––an apartment––that was either rent free or so inexpensive that one could easily afford to live in it. This illustrates the moral universe of Soviet citizens under Stalin. It contains blinders as well as areas of focused attention. Westerners are also attached to their own moral universe. It, too, has its blinders as well as areas of focused attention.

I have cited views about Stalinism by contemporary Russians, as reported by Brian Humphreys. Let us assume, for brevity's sake, that my sketchy citation from Humphrey's article contains at least a grain of truth and validity. It sees Stalinism from the perspective of hardships in Russian life in the mid-1990s. Here a positive rider emerges about the past, as people remember the cheap food, so readily available. They use their imagination––based on the autonomy to imagine and express they now enjoy––to amplify and exaggerate the good aspects of life under Stalin producing, in the view of the reporter, a "growing nostalgia for a life that never really existed." They are operating from the particular current vantage point to create a perspective on the Stalinist past.

In short, we see very different perspectives toward Stalinism. There is the mid-1990s, Russian perspective. It is colored by Russian people's misery, based on the hardships and frustrations they experience now. Given this misery, they are inventing a distorted version of Stalinism, "a life that never really existed." Here in their current immediacy they are producing an idyllic view that conveniently leaves out the horrors and brutalities while, at the same time, emphasizing––perhaps overemphasizing––the satisfactions derived from inexpensive food. Their distance from Stalinism allows them to invent a rosy picture and make that into a new immediacy. It is an immediacy of dreams, tinted by riders.

From their 1990's perspective it is not at all clear what sort of perspective the Russians had toward Stalinism and Communism while they actually lived under it. Humphreys tells us that "by all reports [they] had a less-than-lukewarm relationship with communism while they lived under it."[5]1 shall not attempt to dwell on their perspective at the time of Stalinism except to guess that downtrodden people rarely have the option to entertain grand ideological issues. Bread and butter issues––cheap sausage––loom large. This does not mean that the Russian people did not contribute to the entire political package of Stalinism, offering the lives of their sons to wage its wars as well as their own labors to help implement its various programs. Chances are they did embrace Stalinism with all its horrors––although, perhaps, leaving a bit of room among older individuals for nostalgically dreaming of pre-Stalin Russia and for grumblings within the permitted limits.

The Western perspective to Stalinism is exemplified by Humphreys, who views Russia from the vantage point of being an American reporter. He personifies the Western, anti-Communist perspective. Within that perspective there is the autonomy to confront––intellectually at least–– the horrors of Stalinism. Here is freedom to speak up about the gulag, the deliberate mass starving of the Ukrainian peasants and much more. Yet if we are honest we must acknowledge that this, too, is a decidedly slanted perspective. It is comprised of colorations that derive from the West's conflict with international Communism. It includes some cool assessments of what was actually happening in the Soviet Union under Stalin. But this is coupled with the post-cold war impatience with Russians for not having the infrastructure to embrace Western-style democracy and capitalism––the West's own civic religion, that worships individualism as against collectivism. It, too, is an immediacy of dreams, tinted by riders, made possible by its own distance from Stalinism and its current manufacture of a selective linkage to that past.

NOTE

1 Brian Humphreys, "Tales of cheap sausage and totalitarianism," *The Sun* (Baltimore), June 12, 1996.
2 Ibid.
3 Ibid.
4 Ibid.
5 Ibid.

Exclusivities:
Shadows We Create Over Our Moral Immediacy

> *Morally speaking, are we more advanced than our ancestors? Is there moral progress? Our recent history does not look encouraging. In the pursuit of morality, communities can make profound efforts to instill benign, life-enhancing values and yet, in quest of moral exclusivity, they can foster brutal life-denying values. It can happen by claiming moral superiority over external moralities and, internally, by processes of stern moral purification.*

In the realms of science and technology there surely has been enormous progress. It is evident in the increased sophistication in how we obtain and make use of knowledge about the world in which we live. But in the realm of morality progress remains unclear, to put it mildly.

We have wound up the twentieth century, with its unrivaled episodes of mass slaughter of our fellow human beings. To accomplish this we have harnessed advanced science, developing atomic weapons as well as other, less sophisticated weapons. We have also harnessed some of the crudest hatreds from the past to enroll people into doing horrendous things in the present. In the realm of how humans treat one another on a large scale––country against country, one ethnic group against another ethnic group, one religious group against another religious group ––it looks as though there has been no progress at all. We cannot say with any conviction that we have turned organized human living––in the confines of countries, ethnic communities, even religions––into humane living. When it comes to morality, progress is surely in doubt.

Are we saddled with some sort of sinful nature that inhabits our lives and inflicts permanent inhibitions against moral purification–– and occasionally tempts us to do evil––demonstrating to us that we are flawed and will remain so?

I cannot accept this line of thinking. More likely, I believe, there are inherent pitfalls in how, as entire communities, humans process morality; how we organize the moral system to which we subscribe; how we pursue morality. The pitfalls show up in the fact that in the pursuit of morality we have the disturbing fact that there can be both the profoundest inclination to instill benign, life-enhancing values and, at the same time, the encouragement of some of the most brutal and life-denying values. All in the name of morality; all sponsored by the community.

The brutal life-denying shadows seem to be happening rather consistently and repeatedly. They appear to be endemic and patterned. Therein, amid the horrifics, lies hope. Once we understand the endemic patterning we may, eventually, find ways to gain mastery over them. But first we must understand the patterning.

To illustrate the patterning of these shadows, this tendency to moral pathology that seems to recur over and over again, I shall discuss two aspects of the social processing of morality. One, the frequent delegitimizing of external moralities. Moral systems that differ from our own are devalued, debunked, denied the right to be taken seriously and, even, to exist. Two, the occasional nurturing of ever-more sharply refined moralities *within* existing systems of moral orthodoxy; in the course of this refining of the moral content, morally supported fissures are created within the existing orthodoxy. Both will be shown to create a haunting shadow of moral exclusivity––of one system claiming moral superiority over other moral systems–– while operating within entirely "normal," day-to-day ways of pursuing morality.

De-legitimizing Moralities External to One's Own Community

In the America of the 1990s we saw an effort to spread the message about our form of democracy to other parts of the world. We want to share America's system of morality. We see ourselves as offering a gift to the world: our form of government and societal rule to which we have become accustomed. As America spreads its sphere of influence in the world we see ourselves as largely disinterested, generous contributors to a modern secular religion, the political system we know as democracy––with large realms of personal freedom and dignity, including rights of participation in the political process, in freely following one's religious preferences, in access to economic opportunities. The latter can take the form of actively reaching for and achieving personal wealth. We see the American democratic dream as spreading the word of peace––as we tell ourselves that "democracies don't wage war against one another."

We pay very little attention to the fact that America's particular version of democracy contains a large dose of free-wheeling capitalism and (compared to some other countries) a limited concern for the public good. The focus is on easy access to entrepreneurial activities––to risk- taking in the pursuit of private profit––with relatively limited protection of the public against outright fraud and undermining of the public good. Capitalism is part of America's democratic package for organizing human society. Of course the American package contains many more items––such as those growing out of America's history of accepting very diverse people, who arrived as immigrants and have been accepted into the American compact. I shall not go into these. I merely want to emphasize two things. First, capitalism is woven into the American package of values and commitments. Second, Americans are attempting to spread this package, with a good deal of missionary zeal, to the rest of the world. Americans believe they are doing the world a great favor by spreading the gospel of democracy according to free-wheeling capitalism. Rival secular religions, notably the just-defeated Communism, receive nothing but scorn. During the Cold War when these two secular religions––these two moral systems–– were in confrontation, their respective package of commitments included a large dimension of military arming, preparedness and posturing. Now that Communism has been defeated the military dimension is somewhat diminished, and the economic dimension is vastly increased. (In the year 2016, as this was written, there is renewed military posturing.)

When considering the sense of generosity as America offers its own moral system to the world, one is reminded that over a hundred years ago Britain was spreading the gospel of British imperial rule as a favor to India and many other parts of the world. Seen from within British society, it really did seem that Britain was making a major contribution to a better life for many "backward" peoples. How else could Jawaharlal Nehru manage to study at a British university and, thereby, imbibe the glories of high Western culture before eventually becoming Prime Minister of India? Entirely ignored was the level of arrogance in the denigration of native Indian cultural traditions, and the assumption of moral superiority of Western culture. Britain was doing a favor to "backward" Indians by bringing them within proximity of Western standards of excellence in the art of living a noble life. Surely cricket was a much finer sport than whatever silly games the natives were playing. And beyond India––and beyond playing games––the white man's arrogance justified the virtual killing off, by white settlers, of Tasmanian aboriginals.

The larger issue is that people see their lives in terms of a Local Moral Universe. It defines the nature and meaning of their lives to themselves. It provides moral grounding. It also provides the seeds of moral exclusivity–– that my moral universe is not only different from yours, it is better, truer, more worthy. This happens in city gangs and quasi-religious cults. We also see it in the moral systems under which nations live, just as in the operation of religious cults. Our country's system of morality is superior to theirs The greatest favor we can do "them" is to expose them to our system, with its glorious offerings. The actual content of their system of morality is not worth taking seriously. It is so flawed; it is fundamentally and ultimately worthless. All this may sound simplistic. But it is still at work in our contemporary moral zeal. This is not an exercise in nice abstract discussion. Remember, moral exclusivities have justified the most gruesome acts of warfare. Wars are typically being justified on moral grounds.

Am I advocating a moral relativism or the ultimate multiculturalism–– in which each society is entitled to its own morality–– where, by American and Western standards, China can mistreat the human rights of its citizens and America still accepts China into the world community? Frankly, I do not have a good answer. The question of moral relativism––and the limitation of multiculturalism––is legitimate. But so is the question that addresses the opposite end of the spectrum, the claim to moral exclusivity that assumes moral superiority of our own system, primarily because it is so focused on morality. It is our distinctive vision of the moral universe. It is our local vision, derived from and addressed to our own social community and then applied to the rest of the world.

I began my consideration of Local Moral Universes when I looked into quasireligious cults, and their willingness to sacrifice the lives of their members. It was on display in the mass suicides of cult members near San Diego and at Jonestown. Here were textbook illustrations of systems of locally defined morality that evolved into a total way of life. People were prepared to donate their possessions, their personal skills and energies and their lives to a cause that was defined as infinitely superior to what existed outside the compound in which they had decided to live. Within that system, participants perceived that they were having access to the most transcendent values, to salvation itself. By adhering to the strictures of their messianic leader, they believed they were given a life––and a death––that surpassed, in purity, grace and grandeur, anything they had known before. The sublime was finally within reach. By contrast, the outside world was believed to be in a state of hopeless moral corruption. In its own way, here was the acme of moral exclusivity. One's own system of morality was infinitely superior.

While these cults demonstrate that a Local Moral Universe can generate pathological levels of human behavior, one must also bear in mind that we humans get our sense of self––who we are, what we are––from our connection to a moral context. That connection to a most meaningful moral context can be provided by our country, our religion, our ethnic group, our gender, even our gang. Furthermore, we get what I have called our sense of moral virility from the contribution we actually make to that context. We do so in how we live our lives: "I am an American; I vote and pay my taxes." In short, a Local Moral Universe is a necessary and common social phenomenon. Cults are merely a rather extreme version, a perversion of a common and "normal" pattern.

Since, as a human being, one is so thoroughly wedded to a local moral context––as a contributing member as well as beneficiary of its offerings–– one is very readily tempted into distancing oneself from contrasting moral contexts. One's sense of personal identity is at stake; so is one's sense of the meaning of one's life. Therein lie the rudiments of moral exclusivity–– which is easily exploited by cunning leaders.

A POSTSCRIPT IN THE YEAR 2016

In the 1990's when this section was written I felt justified pointing to modern America as an example of a society offering the world a moral system that claimed superiority over all other moral systems. One heard that "this country has its flaws, but it is the best system that has ever been created" and "this is the First New Nation" namely, the one that embodies the very best of modern, enlightened living. We offered the world a measure of moral exclusivity in the most generous way. We wanted nothing in return, merely that the rest of the world should be wise enough to adopt our moral system.

Alas, in the year 2016 we are witnessing the arrival of ISIS, which claims a measure of moral exclusivity that is infinitely more malignant than America's claims in the 1990's. It is vastly more extreme in its zealotry, that feels justified using murderous terrorism to advance its claim of moral superiority. To be sure it, too, claims to have a vision of the ideal human life. In its own convoluted way, it represents a system of morality. But that system denies the validity of other systems in ways that are so extreme, so fanatical, that any comparison to Modernity, to Enlightenment, is out of the question. It is moral exclusivity in ultimate form.

Nurturing Inward Exclusivities: A Look at Some Religious Issues

When one observes the repetition of orthodox religious practices one might be inclined to think that nothing could be more permanent and stable. It seems that the rituals are being performed precisely as before. They are repeated on rigidly specified occasions and enacted in rigidly specified manner. True enough, but also deceptive. There is less permanence––and less tranquility––than meets the eye.

First, ask any participant whether the previous enactment of the ritual was identical to today's enactment––ask an orthodox Jew whether today's morning service was identical to yesterday's; ask an observant Catholic whether this Sunday's mass was identical to last Sunday's. Both will, indeed, be able to list identical features. Both will also be able to list crucial differences which, to the outside observer, may not have been at all evident. To the immersed, observant congregant, each and every observance of a ritual may seem to be filled with subtle and entirely acceptable freshness, newness, and innovation alongside its comforting reiteration of traditional practice. There is ritual purity, blended with ongoing living. There is creativity, combined with ritual persistence.

Second, consider the diversity among orthodox religious communities. Consider the diversity from church to church, even within the same denomination. Consider the diversity from synagogue to synagogue, again within the same category of orthodoxy. Ask the congregants whether their own congregation is not virtually identical to other congregations in its ways of observing rituals and traditional practices, and they will be able to tell you that they can list substantial differences. From their own vantage point of being observant members of one congregation the differences are apt to seem significant for their own lives. They are living their religious life within one system which, to them, is seen to be an organic unity, containing a vitality and richness of its own, that separates it from adjacent religious congregations, even when, in a formal sense, they belong to the same larger religious association. Individual members will recall how the most vital of their life transitions––the celebration of births, the confrontation of death and serious illness among loved ones–– were addressed in the confines of their religious congregation. These leave indelible marks on one's life, enhancing one's attachment to that particular congregation.

Third, consider how, over time, there is a tendency to develop refinements within existing orthodoxies. This often results in applying highly creative energies to developing ever-more refined distinctions within the existing orthodox tradition. Among orthodox Jews, for example, we see creation of ever-more refinements of dietary rules. What constitutes really kosher foods is under ongoing refinement, where some of today's generation of orthodox Jews will no longer eat in their orthodox parents' home because it is not "kosher enough." What applies to dietary rules applies to other ritual practices as well. There are active, ongoing refinements, being created by fervent adherents to particular religious communities. Each claims high moral ground of close proximity to the transcendent ideals while, at the same time, creating divergences within the existing social community of believers. Each refinement–– be it the latest conception of what kosher really means for observant Jews or the Catholic conception of celibacy of the clergy––is assumed to be timeless and permanent, when in fact it was devised at a particular stage during the historical life of the community of believers.

Here the shadow over moral immediacy takes the form of an ongoing process of creating refinements of the religious rituals, under the most fervent and sincere effort to adhere to an existing system. The process is turned inward, looking for moral renewal within the system.

The ongoing creation of refinements can create morally viewed fissures within the community, which may produce awesome enmities and ruptures among competing interpreters of orthodoxy. In some cases, there is cult-like commitment to particular religious leaders––and their interpretation of what constitutes true orthodoxy––with attendant distancing from anyone who does not share that commitment.

In short, the shadow over moral immediacy can come from the creative dynamism that exists in and around the enactment of traditional rituals. Creativity is focused inward. It is governed by an escalating rider of how rituals are carried out and how they can be made more refined. In this process there can emerge claims of moral purity for one's particular version of the rituals and practices. These can distinguish and separate one's own congregation from other congregations, from non-adherents to a particular spiritual leader and even from one's own kin. Being based on moral idealism, there can arise claims to moral superiority––even claims that I am more morally humble, more ascetic, than you are. Under the claim of moral rectitude, some of the most inhumane actions are being justified. I am thinking of the moral zealotry of Crusaders who, over the objection of some local bishops––their fellow Christians––went on murderous rampages against Jewish communities, all in the name of having a more accurate version of moral rectitude.

My examples have focused on the shadows over the moralisms of religious systems. I could equally have focused on other systems, such as political systems, that also claim moral respectability. Let us recall the moral fervor of political revolutionaries, notably those who carried out the French Revolution. In their zeal these revolutionaries first sent their external enemies to the guillotine. Then they turned against their own members––individuals *within* their fraternity who were not sufficiently zealous––and sent them to the guillotine. Cutting off people's heads seemed an entirely appropriate price to pay for moral shortcomings.

I have pointed to these issues to show that inherently "natural" processes––such as how, over time, creative amplifications and refinements of rituals are apt to develop––can lead to morally sanctioned fissures that pit groups of orthodox persons against one another. Furthermore, such "natural" processes may stand in the way of moral progress. They are apt to generate moral warfare rather than peace, moral rivalries rather than cooperation, moral stalemates rather than progress.

I do not believe that these processes within moral systems are inevitably pernicious. Nor do I believe that the tendency to turn against external moral systems is inevitably pernicious. Yes, they can produce pernicious results. Yes, they use as their building material processes that are entirely understandable and part of the normal workings of human social action. But the very normality of this building material means that it is not beyond our power to comprehend how it works. This, surely, is the first step toward exercising some mastery over it. To this first step I have tried to contribute in this chapter.

The next step is to deliberately focus on these tendencies toward exclusivity and the price we pay for it in the form of zealotry and warfare. With this awareness we can concentrate on ways to avoid the blind pursuit of exclusivity––without giving up claims to honoring separate traditions. In short, we can try to promote a moral federalism. If the American experience with democratic federalism has taught us anything, it is surely that people with different traditions can find ways to respect one another and live together. The hope is that the rough edges of moral exclusivity can be rounded off, so that they do not necessarily create injury and pain for those who are different from ourselves.

Shaping Immediacy––The Particular Ways We Look at the World: *The Case of Gestalt Psychology*

The ways we think––the particular ways we look at the world–– are often shaped by a distinctive configuration of thought (gestalt). Gestalt psychologists alerted us to the reality of such configurations of thought. Their insight became a central intellectual tool of the modern marketing industry.

In this essay I shall dwell on how gestalt thinking can come about: the role of riders, the impingings from and exchanges with an environment and the cybernetic processes which, together, can create and sustain a gestalt.

A major intellectual contribution to psychology comes to us from Gestalt psychology, which came to prominence in the 1930s and has continued to influence our awareness of how we see the world. It represents a point of view that stands in opposition to what is still, surprisingly, a prevailing point of view in psychology as well as in some other sciences. That prevailing point of view is reductionistic: It "attempt(s) to explain a complex interrelated whole in terms of its simpler elements or parts, or in terms of elements belonging to a lower level of phenomena."[1] It is atomistic; it holds to the belief that "something small is more fundamental than something large."[2]

The gestalt point of view goes by a number of different names: wholistic (as against focus on constituent parts); organismic processes (as against focus on mechanical processes[3]); organized complexity (as against simplicity); and field theory––an approach borrowed from physics and applied to psychology, chiefly by Kurt Lewin and his followers (Lewin sees the "field" as "Life Space . . . of interrelatedness of the person and the environment," where "(a)ll psychological events––thinking, acting, dreaming, hoping, et cetera––are conceived to be a function of the life space which consists of the person and the environment viewed as *one* constellation of interdependent factors"[4]); systems theory (that is, entire systems are the "entity" under study); and, of course, gestalt, or configuration.

What all of these have in common is that they regard organized complexities––wholes, organisms, configurations, gestalten, fields––as directly at work, as "actors" in their own right. These complexities, these systems, are not reducible to simpler components. They operate with distinctive and distinguishable processes––notably cybernetic processes––that affect the entire system and which, most importantly, can be understood through the methods of science.

An illustration of Gestalt psychology can be seen in the work of Solomon E. Asch, who was a leading Gestalt psychologist. Here is an example of one of his experiments.[5]

Subjects in Asch's experiments [typically, a group of students] are asked to think about the following passage, and are told that its author is Thomas Jefferson:

"I hold it that a little rebellion, now and then, is a good thing, and as necessary in the political world as storms are in the physical."

When asked whether they agree with the sentiment expressed, and what it really means to them, subjects generally approve it, and interpret the word "rebellion" to mean somewhat minor agitation. But when the subjects are told that the author is Vladimir Lenin, they generally repudiate the statement, and interpret the word "rebellion" to mean violent agitation.

In Asch's opinion, either, (1) Jefferson is associated with being "good" and Lenin being "bad," and therefore when the statement is associated with Jefferson, it is accepted; and when it is associated with Lenin, it is rejected. Both responses are based on one's prejudices and previous opinions. Or, (2) it is believed that if Jefferson wrote the passage he could only have meant by it mild agitation; if Lenin, he surely had in mind violent agitation. Or, a combination of (1) and (2). In each case a rational evaluation leads to the different judgments.

Asch's view is that the individual's judgment is formed by his cognitive processes being shaped by a gestalt, a configuration; the act, the decision to accept or reject the statement is itself part of that gestalt. Each of the two decisions is invoked by a different gestalt, a different configuration of thought. Each configuration is real; each creates the way a person thinks precisely because it molds thinking. Thinking––and acting on the basis of one's thinking—is crucially shaped by such a configuration, such a gestalt. The immediacy— how the individual perceives and responds to a particular statement—is created by that gestalt, by that particular mental configuration.

This raises some questions. How does a gestalt come about? What processes are at work? What are the dynamics in the formation of such a "configuration?"

In the Asch example, the names—Jefferson and Lenin—serve as activating symbols for an entire gestalt. They do so in two steps. Each name, once it is mentioned, activates a distinctive configuration—a package of attitudes and beliefs linked to each named individual. What people think about Jefferson and Lenin suddenly comes alive. Then, most importantly, that distinctive configuration is *brought into* the immediate situation in such a way that it prevails, it dominates the thinking of the individuals in response to the statement the researcher read to them.

In short, the symbols—the names of Jefferson and Lenin—are carriers of a particular piece of reality that they help to import and that then prevails as a rider to the thinking by individuals who respond to the researcher's reading of the statement.

Let me repeat, the symbol in each case serves as the vehicle that accomplishes the connection between a particular piece of external reality, which had been stored in the individual's memory, and the immediate, active reality, in which a decision is being made about the meaning of the statement offered by the researcher. That piece of external reality now shapes the immediacy. It was selectively retrieved from the individual's memory and then implanted into the immediate present in a manner that entirely pervades that immediacy, becoming a cognitive gestalt that dominates the ongoing thinking.

Here is a more concrete example. In cigarette advertising of the last half of the twentieth century a famous athlete, a sexually attractive young woman, or a strong outdoorsman, serves as the vehicle (the connecting symbol) that links a teenager to the message that smoking is a healthy, sexy, tough-and-strong thing to do. We are not dealing with the retrieval of stored memory but instead with the creation of a new configuration of thought, a new gestalt, that is deliberately promoted. But the mechanism is the same as in the gestalt experiment. It is the linkage that creates a particular gestalt, which then leads to a specific response by the individual who has been targeted.

Returning to the Asch example, it deals with two particular cognitive gestalten––that is, each gestalt demonstrates how the world is perceived in response to one statement. It does so on a rather small scale, namely how a few individuals perceive a specific aspect of the world around them.

On a larger scale, I have discussed elsewhere the cognitive gestalt that prevailed in Hitler's Germany. Hitler deliberately implanted the rider of Germany's shame about its loss of World War I––and the need to wash away that shame through his leadership–– thereby negating any opposition to his military adventurism and genocidal racism. That rider crystallized much of the thinking of the German people. Here was an instance of a rider serving as the master symbol bringing a particular cognitive "reality" into play and thereby shaping the entire configuration of German thought, making Germans impervious to other ways of thinking, even when the Nazis engaged in the most atrocious actions under the umbrella of that rider.

However, the sort of cognitive gestalt I have just described is merely the end result of a gestalt-forming process. Energizing and sustaining a gestalt often are an underpinning by self-sustaining and self-regulating processes that can make it impervious to influences outside that system. They firm it up; they insulate it. I am speaking of cybernetic systems that can undergird the gestalt phenomenon.[6]

There are several kinds of cybernetic systems. I shall discuss four of them. Magoroh Maruyama tells us, "Since its inception, cybernetics was more or less identified as a science of self-regulating and equilibrating systems. Thermostats, physiological regulation of body temperature, automatic steering devices, economic and political processes were studied [by cyberneticists] under a general mathematical model of deviation-counteracting feedback networks."[7]

The focus has been on how equilibrium is being maintained through deviation-counteracting processes within a system, where the parts of the system influence each other in ways that keep deviation in check. It is accomplished through feedback mechanisms that selectively activate components of the system that contribute to the state of equilibrium.

Maruyama tells us that in addition to this "first cybernetics," there is a "second cybernetics," in which a deviation-amplifying process prevails. Here the system encourages deviation from its existing structure. Both, deviation counteracting and deviation amplifying are "mutual-causal systems, i.e., the elements within a system influence each other either simultaneously or alternately."[8] In the first cybernetics there is a negative feedback after each deviation; in the second there is positive feedback after each deviation, causing the deviation to grow and grow. Maruyama calls the first type of process, "morphostasis" and the second, "morphogenesis."

Here is an example of morphogenesis. Why did a particular city arise in a particular location in a Middle Eastern desert? Perhaps a trading caravan had to stop because the axle of one of its wagons broke. It took more than a day to repair the axle; hence arrangements had to be made to set up facilities for a more lengthy stay; this led to search for a local supply of water, perhaps even the digging of a well. There began a search for food, perhaps even discovery of relatively nutritious plant life in the vicinity; some individuals found out that they enjoyed gathering local food much more than the frequent travel in the caravan; and so forth. One thing leads to another, each reinforcing the evolving pattern of promoting the group's settling down and creating the conditions for permanent residence. It may have included eventually erecting a religious shrine in celebration of the new form of communal living. Technically speaking, each positive feedback led to another positive feedback, all pointing to "amplifying the deviation" away from the frequent travel mode of living.

Somewhere during this morphogenetic process there emerged the cognitive mindset––the gestalt––that said living in the city is appropriate, valuable and noble. It became a prevailing rider that influenced much of day-to-day life in the city and in the city's relationship to its surroundings.

In all this a relatively small fortuitous event constituted the *initial kick* that set in motion the feedback processes that had a distinctive deviation-amplifying character, eventually producing a city where none had existed before. It happened without specific forward planning. It happened entirely because the components within the system operated in a "mutual-causal" manner that emphasized positive feedback in the direction of settling in the location where the group happened to find itself because of the initial kick. Despite the unplanned, fortuitous nature of this process, it can eventually lead to a mindset that clings to life in this city as an iron-clad necessity, worthy of defense with one's very life.

Morphogenetic systems "are ubiquitous: accumulation of capital in industry, evolution of living organizations, the rise of cultures of various types, interpersonal processes which produce mental illness, international conflicts and the processes that are loosely termed Vicious circles' and 'compound interest'; in short, all processes of mutual causal relationships that amplify an insignificant initial kick, build up deviation and diverge from the initial condition."[9]

In addition to the two types of cybernetics identified by Maruyama—morphostasis and morphogenesis—one can conceive of a third and a fourth type of cybernetics. These can be characterized, respectively, as morphentropics and as morphorigorics. Morphentropics is the type of system (to which Maruyama himself alludes) where, in conformity to the second law of thermodynamics, there is movement toward entropy; the system is on its way to losing its character, its structure, its very existence; the "system" is being replaced by random activity. Deviations are neither counteracted nor amplified. Instead, the deviations influence the system—its very structure—with unconstrained abandon, eventually destroying it altogether.

Morphorigorics is the type of system where rigor mortis is setting in; the system is in a state of decreasing responsiveness to any and every stimulus. Deviations are prevented from taking place. (Whereas in the previous type, the deviations not only take place, they prevail over the system.) The system is frozen into immobility. Here I am reminded of the *Musselmaenner* in the concentration camps. These are individuals who, in the eyes of the observer, have ceased to live even before they have died; they do not respond to anything at all; they are walking dead. Perhaps theirs is a temporary state—of morphorigoris—about to be replaced by the state of morphentropics, that is, total dissolution of their existence through death.

In all four types of cybernetics there appears to be a prevailing rider that shapes both the direction of the entire system and its relationship to its environment.

To be sure the manner in which the rider arrives and manifests itself may vary. In the case of the *Musselmaenner*, it may manifest itself in a final decision—conscious or not—to stop responding to anything at all.

The decision may have been initiated by a fortuitous initial kick––such as dropping one's only food dish; the dish breaks; one is without food; one does not have the energy to go looking for another dish; one's loss of food leads to increasing loss of energy; and so forth. Here begins a deviation-amplifying process. But it is followed by a new emergent consensus, a new rider, that will dominate this system, this life of a human being. It states: Life is not worth living; life is not worth the struggle it takes to keep alive. This decision, once it is planted as a rider, then shapes all actions of the *Musselman*.

Such a fortuitous planting of a rider differs from the case of Nazi Germany where, in speeches by Hitler and in sophisticated propaganda campaigns, the rider of Germany's shame that must be washed away was deliberately planted. In the Asch example, also, the activation of each of the two riders was deliberately planted by the researcher's prodding.

No matter how a particular rider comes about, it seems that each type of cybernetic system can have a distinctive rider that shapes the mindset of people. The mindset links these people to the external world in distinctive ways. Even the *Musselman*, seemingly cut off from the surrounding world, lives under a distinctive "pact" with that world: I won't react to you! At the same time, by renouncing the ongoing struggle with the immediate circumstances around oneself, the *Musselman* may have gained unlimited autonomy to live in an illusory world (for the brief period one will remain "alive"). There are no longer any constraints that have any impact––to show up for the forced inspections or for work details; obedience to camp personnel is no longer regarded as compulsory; physical threats no longer carry any weight. One can dream freely, without interruption or limitation.

Some questions I have not answered:

What sort of rider is involved in morphentropic systems––where the system is entirely open to deviations, but neither reacts against them nor reinforces them; where neither any existing component part nor the entire system is deemed worth defending against attack? Consider an organized group that has just taken a vote to dissolve itself: It has declared that its existence is no longer warranted. A new rider prevails: the group is no longer worth supporting; it no longer exists. Its members can go their separate ways. They are no longer accountable to the group.

In the first two cybernetics, as described by Maruyama, there is a seemingly mechanical bias. Systems react either positively or negatively to deviations. To be sure the reactions tend to have opposite consequences for the system——either they promote deviation (growth) or they inhibit deviation by promoting equilibrium. To be sure, too, an "initial kick" may set the tone for adopting the positive or the negative reaction pattern. But does this necessarily continue? Can there be new kicks, leading into new directions?

Presumably the *Musselman* was not always a *Musselman*. At some point one became a *Musselman*, Or, take the case of ordinary healthy cells in the human body that suddenly turn to a cancerous pattern of unstopping multiplication——deviation-amplifying processes——whereas previously they had limited their multiplication to repair and replacement of tissue that is part of the ongoing, healthy pattern of organic existence. A new directionality seems to be at work in each case. It may have been triggered by a new kick.

Yet the larger issue is that a new governing principle——a new rider—— seems to be guiding the ongoing activities in each of the situations. If my view is correct that each rider retains a distinctive linkage to some external reality, then we may have a clue as to how such new governing principles can arrive on the scene and be accepted. In the case of the *Musselman*, as I have already suggested, that distinctive linkage to the external reality can consist of certain immediacies of one's environment being utterly rejected, whereas others——those in an entirely illusory world——may be firmly embraced. In short, the new system——even though it may exist for only a very short time, it *is* a "system"——is the result of having adopted a new process of exchange with an environment, allowing that environment to impinge in specific morphentropic ways.

In the case of cancerous cells, multiplying with abandon, there appears to be rejection of the constraints ordinarily imposed on cell replication. Perhaps the regulatory mechanisms have become faulty through damage to the DNA or (more likely) through activation of an already-existing DNA aberration. Here, too, there seems to be a turning to a new process of exchange with an environment, where the cancerous cells operate under an entirely new code of communal existence. The neighboring cells can be pushed aside so rudely, so fully, that they can no longer perform their function of helping keep the larger system alive. Presumably the activation of the aberrant DNA is the new prevailing rider that governs the direction of the system, under which the cancerous cells can continually multiply with disregard for their neighbors.

Let us go back to gestalt and the ways we think: It turns out that when new riders prevail they can shape a new immediacy, which defines how we think and act. Each such immediacy will contain a particular gestalt created and perpetuated by a particular cybernetic process—with its own momentum, pushing it into a particular direction. If we stand back we see that the shaping of each immediacy includes an exchange arrangement between a system and its environment, based on a distinctive impingement by that environment which is, then, expressed in a systemic way.

NOTE

1　E. H. Sloane, "Reductionism," *Psychology Review 52* (1945) 214-233. Cited in Martin Scheerer, "Cognitive Theory," in Gardner Lindzey, editor, *Handbook of Social Psychology* (Cambridge, MA: Addison-Wesley, 1954), pp. 91-142.
2　Ibid., p. 93.
3　"Organismic" need not refer only to biological organisms. The philosopher and mathematician Alfred North Whitehead developed a theory about the physical universe that he calls organismic.
4　Morton Deutsch, "Field Theory in Social Psychology," in Gardner Lindzey, editor, *Handbook of Social Psychology*, p. 185.
5　The following is based on Gordon Allport's article, "The Historical Background of Modern Social Psychology," in Gardner Lindzey, editor, *Handbook of Social Psychology*, (Cambridge, MA: Addison-Wesley, 1956) p. 28. Allport cites from S. E. Asch, *Social Psychology (New York*: Prentice Hall, 1952), pp. 419-425.
6　The following discussion is heavily indebted to Magoroh Maruyama, "The Second Cybernetics: Deviation-Amplifying Mutual Causal Processes," in Fred Emil Katz, editor, *Contemporary Sociological Theory* (New York: Random House, 1971), pp. 248-262.
7　Ibid., p. 248.
8　Ibid., p. 249.
9　Ibid.

Transformations of Immediacy: Introduction

The immediate world in which we live can be transformed in subtle ways. The essays in the following section investigate transformations in the confines of an individual's personal career and, on a larger scale, in the confines of a society's social order.

Transformation in the confines of an individual's career is explored in the essay, "Escalating Dualities." Its theme is that personal careers often contain a hidden dimension—a second path—in addition to the dimension that is publicly acknowledged. The second path can include those items which the individual may regard as too painful, too dangerous, too inappropriate to mention openly or to acknowledge to oneself. Still, these items may exist, persist, and even continue to grow, in their subterranean ways. They may on occasion erupt into the open, sometimes producing devastating transformations in the life of the individual. These issues will be illustrated from the careers of military officers, Holocaust survivors who became eminent writers but eventually committed suicide, and the realm of sexuality—where the discussion leads to some revision of the Freudian view of the workings of the unconscious (specifically, I suggest that the unconscious – I call it the subconscious -- may be fed continuously, from one's current experiences, rather than merely result from early life experiences).

The essay, "Moral Mutation - The Immediacy of Tomorrow?" uses the horrors of trench warfare during World War I to raise a question that is not usually asked: Morally speaking, what are the long-term consequences of such horrors? Are the horrors of face-to-face killings on a huge scale, lasting over a considerable period of time surpassed by an even greater horror, the creation of a moral mutation that justifies such killings on moral grounds and is, then, part of the West's heritage that is easily invoked again? Is this the kind of mutation that has permanently transformed our heritage?

How might a society abandon such a mutation? I have not answered these questions. At this point I hope, merely, that I have shown their urgency.

The essay "Switchings: Wrenching Reconfigurations in Immediacy" addresses a seemingly incongruous fact. On the one hand, people often act on the basis of a particular fixed point of view, and that point of view can be utterly impervious to other points of view. It is a complete and full perspective. It tolerates no dissent, no departure from the prevailing perspective.

On the other hand, there can be an abrupt and total switching of point of view. It can happen quite suddenly. The explanation lies, I believe, in the activation of dormant values—values that may have appeared to be entirely absent from people's repertoire, but actually exist in an inactive, dormant state. They are suddenly activated by a particular event. These newly activated values may then totally transform the prevailing ways of thinking and behaving. The very same people who were firm adherents to a particular point of view are now, sometimes suddenly and vehemently, adherents to an entirely different point of view. A new immediacy has come into existence.

The essay, "Fusions that Create a New Immediacy: A Look at Some Aspects of the Spanish Inquisition," also deals with the advent of new immediacy. It takes a well-respected scholar's study of the persecution of Jews during the Spanish Inquisition as a starting point for illustrating the role of riders in serving as both catalysts and steering agents for social transformation.

In a particular variant of the self-fulfilling prophecy, the rider that guided a process of change may, on shepherding that change, itself become sanctified and unassailable orthodoxy. In the case of the Inquisition, brutal anti-Semitism played this role. It moved from being a convenient vehicle for bringing about social changes to becoming a central and unassailable piece of national orthodoxy—to be repeated in Germany in the Nazi era.

Along the way, the essay points to the vulnerability of seemingly well-assimilated people who had been part of the cultural mainstream for decades and even centuries. It can happen when discredited social values persist in a dormant state. With deliberate effort these dormancies may be activated and, drawing on energized moral persuasiveness, transform the existing immediacy. Here the lives of people who thought that they had reached safety by immersing themselves into the mainstream of the society are abruptly turned into social and moral pariahs. Suddenly these people are deemed to be ripe for social exclusion and worse.

(For me, this is personal. My parents, highly assimilated German Jews, were murdered in the Holocaust – as long dormant German anti-Semitism was gruesomely resurrected.)

The Second Path in the Course of Personal Careers:
Escalating Dualities

Personal careers can contain a duality consisting of the individual's publicly visible career path and, behind it, a second path that contains the careerist's unmentionables – the fears, rage, uncertainties, inappropriate honesty, and more. These can occasionally erupt into open immediacy and transform the career unpredictably and destructively.

My first inkling of this phenomenon took place when I was serving in the U.S. Army in the 1950s. I was an enlisted man, assigned to an administrative unit in the army's Infantry School at Ft. Benning, Georgia. This military installation was an advanced training center––more like a university––where officers took refresher programs at a high level of sophistication, critical to their careers in the infantry. My job included keeping records on the performance of officers who were taking courses. It was somewhat incongruous. I, a lowly enlisted man serving as a clerk, was keeping records on officers who ranged in rank all the way up to general.

The officers were individuals who had made service in the army their professional career. Many of them had attained senior positions following service in a variety of military campaigns. They frequently visited the office where their records were kept and inquired about their grades.

It struck me that these individuals––who often had distinguished career achievements behind them and were, even now, holding down highly regarded positions––were exceedingly fearful about their grades. It seemed that anything less than a very high score on the tests was totally crushing to them. They were apprehensive, anxious, worried. These were senior officers in the army. They were men of high accomplishment who, ordinarily, had considerable confidence, sophistication and poise. Yet here all their confidence, sophistication and poise seemed to desert them. They acted as though their entire career was in jeopardy.

Of course there may have been some reality to their apprehensiveness. Promotion to the next rank or getting a coveted new assignment might, indeed, be affected by their test scores. But it seemed to me——entirely intuitively, to be sure——that these men were simply terribly and inordinately scared; that they were elevating that molehill of performance on a single course into a major mountain.

As I now see it, it seems that the officers' increasing confidence, sophistication and poise, nurtured and developed over the years of a successful career was just one dimension in their lives. Perhaps alongside the growth in their confidence, sophistication and poise there might also have been a parallel, though subterranean, growth of apprehension and fear. This second dimension——the obverse of their publicly visible career manifestations——was ordinarily dormant and hidden. But it could, on occasion, erupt into the open.

Stated differently, as the officers advanced in their careers, they were playing for ever-higher stakes. They were engaged in more responsible and rewarding endeavors. But appropriate opportunities became more limited. After all, the career pyramid gets very narrow at the top. There is only one chief of the U.S. armed forces. In any race for that coveted top spot, there are bound to be losers. In deciding who will get to occupy the very few positions near the top, some——the majority of those eligible——are going to be left out. It is very likely to be the ones with the slightly lower score on the test—— even if it is a score on a ridiculous little course. It may give those above you, who will make the decision about your fate, an iota of data for deciding among competing candidates, all of whom are deservedly distinguished, outstanding officers, and entirely qualified for advancement.

In short, there is some reality in this madness. But there also seems to be an accompanying reality of ever-more subterranean fear that one's entire career might be blemished. Everything one has worked for so carefully and for so long would be for naught if one failed to get that final promotion. To validate what one has done, what one has been striving to achieve for such a long time, one absolutely must reach the next higher rung on the ladder. Most important, one's reaching that rung could be derailed by even the most minor of missteps.

On the surface it seems that the officers' career evolution was necessarily accompanied by more confidence, sophistication and poise. But its obverse——the uncertainties, the fear of failure and missteps——may grow alongside the public posture. These attributes, too, may keep pace with the career's evolution, growing apace with it. They are not likely to be the same sorts of fears that the young military officer experienced at the beginning of that career. Instead, these fears are appropriate to the stage of the career in which one now finds oneself. They have grown alongside the career's evolution; they are career-stage specific. But, if anything, they may be more terrifying than the youthful terrors in the early stages of the career. There is far greater sophistication about the pitfalls and dangers to one's reputation and one's future.

Fears and sense of terror are rarely allowed to be acknowledged or expressed by highly successful persons. But on occasion they can erupt–– sometimes in the sudden resignation from a stable and assured position when one has been denied the recognition one feels one deserves; sometimes in the sudden heart attack that is frequent among career-oriented men––of course women are very likely to catch up, as careerism takes hold in their lives.

My second inkling of the subterranean growth of discordant unmentionables ––what I am calling the second path in an individual's career––came on hearing about the suicide of a number of highly successful Holocaust survivors. Among these were the following writers: Primo Levi, Jerzy Kosinski, Tadeusz Borowski, Paul Celan, Jean Amery and Bruno Bettelheim.

Here were persons who had evidently found a way to lead a meaningful and productive life after their own survival of horrors in the Holocaust. Yet they eventually, after their apparently successful return to a productive and rewarding and meaningful life, committed suicide.

One of these was Primo Levi. After Auschwitz he briefly resumed his career as a chemist. But he soon turned to writing––and what a writer he became! He wrote about his experiences at the concentration camp. But this was not as a survivor who wallowed in suffering, who reiterated the horror of the horrors. He wrote as a participant who was there and as a scientist who observes and reflects. He gave us poignancy about specific events and transcending insights that went beyond the individual events. He showed us the unique and the universal. He created balance between acknowledging life-denying horrors and life-affirming human dignity asserting itself amid the horrors. He created discernment that seemed to raise him above the beguilings of evil.

Beyond his writings about the events of Auschwitz, he turned to writings that had little to do with the woes of human existence and much to do with the celebration of life. He wrote of the joys of nature; he wrote of the world of science, where his fine-toned spirituality softened the harsh impersonality of scientific reasoning. It seemed that Levi had found a way to celebrate the vibrancy of life. That he had discovered for himself––and for the rest of us––ways to enjoy and celebrate membership in the human community. He had done so through the healthy process of becoming a creative and active contributor to that community's zest for life.

Yet this man committed suicide. And he was not alone. As I began to investigate, it became disconcertingly clear that a number of Holocaust survivors who had become highly successful people committed suicide. What is going on here? Perhaps, as my friend, the writer Henryk Grynberg states, these individuals had never really "survived" the horrors. To be sure they survived physically. But emotionally and psychically, they had not survived; their early pain remained. The life-denyings continued within them. They could never cleanse themselves of the poison planted in their soul.

A different explanation may be that among these individuals, just as among the army officers, there was actually an internally escalating process that was the very obverse of their public career. That despite their outward success in leading a successful and satisfying life, their subterranean sense of vulnerability, pervasive fear, and terror had not only not ended. It grew as a path that had a life of its own––although it remained largely hidden. Over time that second path reached such potency that it eventually erupted, asserting its dominance in the individual's psyche. It then expressed itself in the final act of total despair: suicide.

Stated a bit more psychologically, perhaps we can relate the phenomenon to the Freudian vision of the unconscious, but revise it to focus on the subconscious. Sigmund Freud saw the unconscious as being part of one's personality that is largely hidden from one's conscious awareness. It is also of long standing––it is usually due, in Freud's view, to very early life experiences. The task of psychoanalysis, Freud told us, is to retrace and rediscover these early, damaging experiences. I suggest that the second part of this formulation may need to be amended.

Namely, there is a subconscious–– a hidden part of one's personality that can be fed continually from one's ongoing life with items that are now disagreeable and frightening. That as part of our daily living we are continually shunting some new items into a hidden niche––the subconscious––because they are unacceptable and dangerous to ourselves, as we ourselves perceive them. In the case of the Holocaust survivors who became successful, it is surely an error to assume that all facets of their post-Holocaust lives were comfortable, cozy, and satisfying. Instead, being nuanced and sensitive people, they could perceive many fearsome elements in their present life. What were these?

It is conceivable that their survivor guilt kept on growing as their worldly success kept on growing. It aroused their increasing feelings of accountability to those who did not survive. Were their successes––their awards, their financial affluence––telling them that they were dancing on the graves of their loved ones? As their success increased, so may have their sense of dissonant linkage to those who were left to die, creating dangerous fragility within themselves.

Fragility is not unique to survivors of horrors. It also exists in the careers of persons where we least expect it, among highly successful persons. A John Adams, a Winston Churchill, an Albert Einstein––their private lives suggest that they acutely felt many hurts they had to absorb. To my knowledge, Einstein did not die a happy man.

I am reminded of a televised interview with Walter Cronkite,[1] the retired television news anchorman. During his tenure as the premier CBS news anchorman, he was by far the most respected of newscasters. For about two decades, millions of viewers routinely turned on their television to receive news whose reliability they felt they could trust, because it was brought by a man they trusted. To say that Walter Cronkite was respected is an understatement. For millions of people he was deeply venerated –– and still is, long after his death.

Yet in the interview, conducted during his eightieth year, Cronkite expressed the most pitiful hurt about being slighted by the television network he had served so long. Nowadays, he says, they do not invite him to their receptions and parties. He is made to feel unwelcome when he visits the newsroom where he used to work. This revered man expressed such pain, such agony, that it is truly astounding. Here is a man who has earned the highest respect from millions of people. Yet he now feels terribly hurt when a few people––people of infinitely less accomplishment than his own––do not show him respect. How could such a man––a man of such poise, sobriety, and strength––be so vulnerable?

As a rule highly respected people do not acknowledge their fears and vulnerabilities in public. At least, not during their tenure in highly esteemed roles, where protective walls insulate the occupant from confronting their personal vulnerabilities. In the case of the interview with Cronkite, we are seeing him in retirement from the esteemed role, no longer insulated by a protective wall. Furthermore, the interview itself was conducted by a tabloid-type of program––the sort of program that Cronkite would have shunned during his tenure as esteemed journalist. There, in the course of the interview, his emotional vulnerabilities were deliberately milked. There, his pain was exploited. The interviewer claims to show the "human" side of this noble man while, in fact, stripping him of his humanity by displaying to all of us that he, too, has a fearful inner side which, at the age of eighty, may be more raw and vulnerable than ever.

Look at the life of any adult––ordinary people, not just famous people such as Mr. Cronkite––is there not diminished autonomy to admit weakness, to express fears and uncertainties, as compared to the child? Might these uncertainties and fears be placed in subconscious storage from which they may inadvertently and unexpectedly erupt? When and how are they likely to erupt? When and how are they likely to be stored safely? When and how are they routinely dissipated and not stored at all? Similarly, in the life of leaders and persons of high status generally: Are these individuals not limited in the autonomy to admit weakness and uncertainty–– even to themselves, but more so to those around them?

In a traditional, one-career family the spouse––usually the wife––often served as the receptacle for the male careerist's work-related frustrations, fears and rage. To his wife he could safely voice these career-negatives without worry that they would be communicated to his career peers. With the advent of two-career families, this safety valve has largely disappeared. There is rarely room for two sets of career frustrations to be vented and receive nurturent acknowledgment. More than ever, it seems, the second path remains dangerously repressed, awaiting explosive eruption.

Returning to the Freudian notion of the unconscious: that the unconscious component of the individual's psyche is largely rooted in very early experiences in life that have never been resolved and, consequently, raise their ugly head occasionally. The unconscious can be aroused—usually in destructive ways—by current events in the individual's life, but basically it is made up of long-buried experiences. How realistic is this? Can one reduce the pain of the eighty-year-old Walter Cronkite to unresolved early childhood experiences that remained buried inside? Surely, this is stretching credulity.

By contrast, I suggest that a subconscious can be created— even newly created—and continually nurtured in the ongoing life of adults. The individual's present life—the here and now—can contain elements that are continually shunted aside into a location that is a hiding place from the individual's current public face. It can, for example, contain elements of total terror that an apparently self-confident individual would be loath to admit, even to oneself. This terror may not be a childhood terror, as the Freudians might picture it, but an entirely adult terror, based on real—but unmentionable— interpretations of circumstances in the individual's present life. In the case of Walter Cronkite, the insults to his person were perpetrated after the zenith of his career. There was vulnerability. The dagger hit its mark. It had spotted a current weakness.

What is unusual about the Walter Cronkite case is that the pain's impact was revealed in full public view. Ordinarily such pain is carefully hidden. It is shunted into a siding where neither the public nor oneself is allowed to be fully conscious of what is happening. Only in one's dreams does one occasionally dare to confront such pain. There, too, it tends to arrive in veiled forms that make it difficult to understand the source and its precise impingement on our current ways of living.

As Freud taught many of us, the world of dreams is often the actively displayed version of the unconscious. One might call it the second path of our existence. When we read the biblical story of Jacob's wrestling with God's representative during the night, we are shown the unsettling restlessness that can gain the upper hand during the night.[2] We may experience night's limitlessly wondrous side as well as its unconstrainedly fearsome side. Here "nighttime work"—with its profound wrestling with one's conscience, its occasional eruptions of total terror—contrasts sharply with "daytime work," where, the theologian Walter Bruegeman tells us, humans may seem to have control over their destiny. "During the day, [Jacob] is able to manage and take initiative. But at night, as for all of us, Jacob turns out to be vulnerable, and things rush powerfully beyond his control. His night is peopled by those uninvited and unwelcome in his life. But they are the very ones with whom he has to come to terms, if he is to go home peaceably."[3] Here the second path, the duality of our existence, is in full view.

A third inkling about the second path comes from the relations between blacks and whites in America of the 1990s. Glenn Loury, a distinguished black economist writers: "Arguably, the most race-obsessed people in America today are not Southern rednecks but rather the well-educated and prosperous black elites."[4]

This bears out my own impression––unscientifically gathered, but convincing to me––that many blacks who, by general American standards, are highly successful, seem to be the most despairing. These are persons who, in their personal careers, in their standard of living, in economic terms and in educational terms, are highly successful. Yet they seem to feel fiercely that they are being denied their full and rightful place by the white race––a race with whose members they now have the closest of contact.

Loury's explanation is that the members of the black middle class are finally having a chance to express themselves and be heard by their former oppressors––who are now "not strangers, but . . . neighbors and coworkers . . . . For the first time, they engage their oppressors in moral discourse as political equals." It gives these blacks "a greater opportunity to express the racial injustices they still feel."

This is surely plausible. But it does not seem to account for the high level of race obsession among these "advantaged" blacks that Loury himself recognizes. It does not seem to account for the seemingly high level of despair, anger, feeling bereft, that is being felt and expressed by these persons. It seems to me that their anguish refers not merely to those blacks who are still disadvantaged––who live in poverty and high crime districts in the cities, and who (in Loury's words) make up a disproportionately large share of the underclass. It does not seem to account for their memory of past horrors inflicted historically on blacks.

On the contrary, they seem to be speaking of their own situation. Of their own lives. Of here and now. How can this be?

It seems to me that for many of these successful blacks the route to economic success has been beset by difficulties. It is a route where the successful black professional––the physician, the lawyer, the college professor––must answer the spoken or unspoken query: Are you an affirmative action product? Who would want to be treated by a physician who did not "earn" medical credentials, except through the social charity of affirmative action? Such denigrations are probably common and are part of the burden borne by many a black professional. (Of course the other variant of this pattern, nowadays conveniently ignored, is that traditionally disadvantaged categories of individuals––women, Jews, as well as blacks–– who fought to attain social and economic accomplishment before the advent of affirmative action, had to be better than those who were habitually given easy access to and preferential treatment for admission to elite universities and occupations.)

I have cited just one item––the accusation of being an affirmative action product––in the memory of the black person who has struggled to achieve the American dream. Surely there are many more items, to all of which a black individual can be acutely sensitive.

It seems to me that the memory of racial struggles in the course of one's own career can attain a dormant life of its own––paralleling the life of the Holocaust survivor's painful experiences––where the pain is not only not extinguished, once and for all, but may actually keep on being fed, smolder painfully and cancerously expand, though in subterranean fashion. Here, as in the life of the military officers whom I met at Ft. Benning, the more successful one is in one's publicly visible career, the more the uncertainties, fears and misgivings may continue to be fed, persist and grow in the form of a second path that exists beneath the surface. And, as in the case of these military officers, it seems that precisely when the black middle class person becomes more and more "successful," in the terms of American middle-class expectations, the stakes seem to become not only higher but ever more precarious. Each and every slight from a white colleague, even when unrecognized and unintended by that colleague, can easily be magnified into a major insult. The result can be anguished actions that are truly destructive to one's life.[5]

Another case of the second path: the case of a famous British actress and her demons. Glenda Jackson, formerly a highly acclaimed actress, later a member of Parliament: "Jackson, who has two Best Actress Oscars, and was a 1972 Emmy winner . . . walked away from movie celebrity in 1992 and won election . . . [to Parliament]. During a twenty-seven-year acting career, she suffered from extreme stage fright; she told the *Guardian* last September that "the longer I carried on, the greater the fear became.""

Yet another connection of Freud's work to the second path: the issue of sexuality. Freud drew attention to untamed sexuality that was largely covered up in the polite Viennese society of his time. His thesis was that many neurotic illnesses of individuals had their roots in early childhood sexual experiences that were later repressed, but surfaced occasionally in the form of socially inappropriate and neurotic behavior.

Freud left us with an awareness of pervasive sexuality in human beings that is diffused and sublimated in many ways. Most generally, the sexuality is tamed by being funneled into approved social roles, such as marital roles and, more contemporaneously, relatively long-lasting relationships. It is also tamed through elaborate belief systems that emphasize that unrestrained sexuality is largely attributable to raging hormones that are especially pervasive during the period of youth and which, sooner or later, are supposedly outgrown as the individual enters into "responsible" adult social roles. There sexuality is socially controlled and harnessed for the procreation and care of the next generation and sublimated in the decorum governing dealings among adults. Roughly speaking, we may call this the sexuality in the first path.

Now, some consideration of sexuality in the second path.

If we assume that sexuality in humans is relatively permanent, we must open up the possibility that, throughout the individual's life, there is continuing and ongoing input into, and output from the individual's sexuality— and these come not only from biology (namely, hormones) but also from, and to the social environment, whose culture is pervaded by sexual themes.

In the course of daily life there are many sexually tinged transactions in everyday activities. There are interactions with many individuals who can be potential sexual partners. There is exposure to a culture, notably American culture, where sexuality is pervasively used in the marketplace to promote goods and services. All this cannot fail to link up with the individual's reservoir of sexuality.

Given the existing societal rules about appropriate expression of sexuality, there is also an ongoing process of covering up that input when it is deemed socially inappropriate. After all, it is potentially disruptive to the individual's existing social relationships and responsibilities. Yet the culturally supported sexual tiliations continue, and so do the personal cover-ups.

In short, there is an ongoing build-up of sexual dissonance, of culturally sponsored sexual schizophrenia. There is an ongoing input of sexual experience that is both socially sponsored and induced and, at the same time, defined as inappropriate if expressed too openly. This input can often be stored––and re-channeled––relatively safely. But it may also build up in a way that shows up precisely in the form of neuroses and dysfunctional behavior as Freud so accurately noted––what I would call the occasional intrusion of the second path into everyday life. I differ from Freud, however, in emphasizing that sexual experiences defined as inappropriate can be both generated and continually enhanced in adulthood. It can happen in the course of regular adult living as it is offered to us in our society.

In a larger sense, the so-called untamed sexuality of youth as well as the life-long sexuality of human adults may well have its evolutionary roots in an underlying biological reality that has persisted over eons of time and has left an imprint on how we lead our lives. After our birth two contrasting processes appear to operate. Namely, alongside the development of our individuation, in the form of a new and separate life––particularly after childhood, when we are identified as full-fledged separate and independent creatures––there remains a quest for bonding, that seeks comfort and security through closeness and intimacy with another human being; we humans lead individual lives but we are not fully self-sufficient creatures. The biological imperative seems to be that we have inherited a fundamental duality, a quest for separation and a quest for fusion. Perhaps the dual paths in our personal lives are a way of coping with that dual inheritance––with its discordant messages and yearnings.

I have described patterns of escalating dualities that seem to afflict at least some individuals. I do not suggest that such patterns are bound to happen to every human being. Not every high ranking military officer is so afflicted. Not every Holocaust survivor is afflicted with the dormant but escalating pain to the point of eventually committing suicide, or even being seriously tempted to commit suicide. Not every successful black middle-class American is afflicted with ever-expanding——though subterranean——racist disenchantment. Not every adult is afflicted with sexually derived neuroses——as suggested by Freud——but whose sources are adult, rather than childhood, experiences. I do not know how prevalent is the pattern——the second path——I have described. Yet when it does occur it constitutes a potentially explosive compound that may suddenly erupt and intrude into the immediacy of the life of an individual, transforming it drastically.

• • •

Furthermore, the second path may not be at all unhealthy or pathological. To be sure it is made up of items the individual regards as inappropriate for bringing out into the open in the situation in which one now finds oneself. These items are shunted into a silent siding, perhaps permanently, perhaps temporarily. Yet these shunted items may be the most honest, the most moral, the healthiest responses to the reality in which the individual currently operates!

George Lee Butler comes to mind. Since his retirement from the U.S. Air Force he has been the leading organizer of an effort to fully eliminate nuclear weapons on our planet.[7] He has assembled support from leading figures in many countries. Butler is a retired general. During his active duty he commanded America's nuclear forces. While he was the general in charge of these forces he obviously could not advocate——publicly or privately——the elimination of these weapons. But surely he held views about the terrible dangers and inherent uselessness of these weapons for promoting a humane world long before his retirement from the military services. The views had to be kept in silent storage while he commanded America's nuclear forces. After leaving his post in the military service, he is free to tell us:

"We continue to espouse [nuclear] deterrence as if it were now an infallible panacea. And worse, others are listening, have converted to our theology, are building their [nuclear] arsenals, are poised to rekindle the nuclear arms race——and reawaken the specter of nuclear war . . . we have won . . . the opportunity to reset mankind's moral compass, to renew belief in a world free from fear and deprivation, to win global affirmation for the sanctity of life, the right of liberty and the opportunity to pursue a joyous existence."[8]

One is reminded of Dwight Eisenhower's warnings against the "military industrial complex" as he was about to leave office, after a highly distinguished career as both military officer and president of the United States. It is not known why he did not make such a statement during his term in high office. What we do know is that he made the statement——the only one of its kind by him, as far as I know——only as he was *leaving* office as president. Presumably he felt he was in no position to voice these views during his career in high office.

Another president, Lyndon B. Johnson, was eventually run out of office by the increasing unpopularity of America's involvement in the Vietnam War. He vehemently defended America's role in that war. Increasingly he was personally blamed for escalating that conflict. He was depicted as the very personification of a wicked course of action. Day after day there were demonstrations that attacked him for sending hundreds of thousands of American troops into a war that seemed not only un-winnable but increasingly unjustified on both pragmatic political and moral grounds. The outcry against Johnson reached giant proportions, forcing him to turn away from running for a second term as president.

Yet years later the records reveal that Johnson had grave misgivings about the Vietnam War, even while he was publicly defending it. Indeed, he essentially shared the views of his critics—— that it was not worth fighting, that it was morally indefensible. He held these views even before he entered into the process of escalating the number of American troops he was sending into the war. In his public pronouncements Johnson continued to strongly defend America's involvement. In his public actions, he increased America's participation in that war. Yet in his private world, in his second path, he was totally appalled by the war and America's participation in it. While publicly, he appeared to be self-assured and unflinching in his support of the war, he confided in private to his friend, Senator Richard Russell, the chairman of the Senate Armed Services Committee, "We're in the quicksands up to our neck, and I just don't know what the hell to do about it."[9] This was in May 1964, before the largest build-up of American troops. That day, too, he told his national security advisor, McGeorge Bundy, "I don't think it's worth fighting for, and I don't think we can get out." Despite the increasing public outcry against the war, the president was even more afraid of the Congress––"they'd impeach a President, though, that would run out [and abandon the Vietnam war], wouldn't they?"[10] In that situation, says a commentator, "No president can be seen as vacillating. He had to be seen as prudent but also as a strong anti-Communist."[11]

In the case of President Johnson we are having access to information about his second path, thanks to tapes released by the LBJ Presidential Library. That second path was carefully shielded from the public. Indeed, its converse––the self-assured escalator of the war––grew in the public's eye. Yet the second path also grew, receiving input daily and becoming ever more stressful to its owner.

The Second Path: Internal Dynamics

There is every indication that the second path is far more than a mere storage area, a repository, for elements in the individual's life that are publicly unmentionable, deemed personally embarrassing, hurtful, or inappropriate––and which may, on occasion, suddenly erupt into public view, spilling over into the individual's first path. In addition, in all likelihood the second path has internal processes of its own. It contains dynamics; it can be a system in its own right.

First of all, let us bear in mind that the content of the second path is likely to be made up of items from the individual's life that have not been resolved, have not been openly confronted, but are still very much alive and available for interplay with other, unresolved items from life experiences. Hence, we may find seemingly incongruous linkages and interplays–– where time, as we usually think of it, may be entirely disregarded,[12] being replaced by matched experiences from entirely "separate" epochs.

For example, let us look at elderly occupants of a nursing home. Here bewilderings from one's childhood may be linked with bewilderings from one's current geriatric existence in that nursing home––since, in many ways, one is again being treated as a child. One's public routines––one's first path––in the nursing home may be carried out against the not-so-subtle internal battles nurtured by these two sets of bewilderings, each reinforcing the other. This happens even though one of the bewilderings occurred many years ago, and the other, although it is of recent origin, cannot be acknowledged if one is to retain some dignity as a fully functioning adult. The two bewilderings may form a mutually reinforcing system of alienation and disorientation from the nursing home in which the individual now resides.

Beyond such a particular example we must ask, what sort of "systemic" processes are apt to be at work within the individual's second path and which may spill over into that individual's first path, one's publicly acknowledged life? The best approach may be through cybernetics, the science of self-regulating systems,[13] which looks at systems that operate entirely on the basis of their own internal dynamics.

In another section of this book I discuss four kinds of cybernetic systems, each containing a system's self-escalatings brought on by the interaction of its component parts. The first cybernetic is one where equilibrium is being maintained; there are feedback processes, operating within the system, that keep the system in balance by counteracting any drastic disturbances. The second cybernetic promotes growth; here, too, there are feedback processes, within the system, but they serve to keep the system growing. The third cybernetic is where the system is frozen into rigidity; it is not responsive at all; if there are feedback processes within the system, they serve only to inhibit responsiveness. The fourth cybernetic (the opposite of the third) is where there is extreme responsiveness–– to each and every stimulus––leading to emergence of entropy and the system's dissolution; if there are feedback processes, they serve only to escalate responsiveness, until the system is destroyed through exhaustion and dissipation.

In terms of the individual's personality and functioning as an individual, the first cybernetics can promote equanimity. Here the second path handles un-confronted pains and discordant experiences in ways that ensure that they will not spill over into the first path; they are so smoothly controlled that they are not likely to erupt in system-disrupting ways. Similarly, in the second cybernetics, there are no system disruptions. There is, however, expanding capability to handle pain and discordant experiences. In popular language, we then talk about a person becoming increasingly "mature" enough to handle adversity, to accept discordant elements without being destructively distraught about it. In the third cybernetics things change. The frozen rigidity, as in the case of the *Musselman* in the concentration camps,[14] is very likely to destroy the system of individual human beings––both their first and second paths––and their capacity to function at all. It opens the way to the fourth cybernetic, the process of actual dissolution of the system, where entropy takes over and, where once existed a system, sheer randomness will take over.

I suspect that the Holocaust survivors who became successful as writers but ended their life through suicide went through a period of growth (the second cybernetics) where their personality widened as they went through a period of writing about life-affirming matters. They seemed to have reached a way of leading a satisfying and rewarding life. All this was in their first path. In their second path, concomitantly, there grew a second cybernetic version of the obverse attributes; the life-denyings expanded and mutually reinforced each other, being fed by the very successes that marked the first path's seeming health. Each award, each new public acclaim only reinforced one's self-doubt and sense of betraying those who were no longer here to accept acclaim and success. All this finally erupted by transformation of second cybernetics into a fourth cybernetic pattern––extreme responsiveness to issues they had carefully avoided until that moment––bringing with it the total destruction of one's self. (I do not know precisely how––when, triggered by which events––the transformation took place in the life of these writers.)[15]

As this illustrates, the transformation of a second path's second cybernetic into a fourth cybernetic can be destructive to the individual's first path and, on occasion, to life itself. The second path, instead of serving as a safety valve for the first path––of storing items the first path cannot handle––that second path now becomes a threatening force that may annihilate that first path. This raises new questions: When does such a transformation take place? When does the conflict between the first and second paths make life in that immediacy untenable? At this point I do not have the answers. I only have urgent questions.[16]

NOTE

1   Aired December 3, 1996.
2   Walter Bruegemann, "The Struggle Toward Reconciliation," in Bill Moyers, editor, *Talking about Genesis: A Resource Guide* (New York: Doubleday), 1996). Copyright, Public Affairs Television.
3   Ibid., p. 133.
4   Glenn Loury, "The Crisis of Color Consciousness," *The Washington Post,* July 21, 1996.
5   Paul M. Barrett, *The Good Black: A True Story of Race in America* (New York: Dutton, 1998). This book relates the story of a highly accomplished black lawyer, going from his beginnings in a housing project, to Harvard Law School, to a prominent law firm, to a crushing end over issues of perceived racial discrimination which, to an outsider, might not appear to be acts of discrimination.
6   Cited from *Time* magazine, February 24, 1997, p. 27.
7   George Lee Butler, "Scrap nuclear weapons––all of them," *The Baltimore Sun*, February 4, 1997. This article is adapted from a speech given January 8, 1997, at the Henry L. Stimson Center in Washington.
8   Ibid.
9   "Tapes that show LBJ tormented by escalation of war," *The Baltimore Sun,* February 15, 1997.
10 Ibid.
11 Ibid.
12 For an intriguing look at "time" see, Alan Lightman, *Einstein's Dreams* (New York: Warner Books, 1993).
13 Magoroh Maruyama, "The Second Cybernetics: Deviation-Amplifying Mutual Causal Processes," in Fred Emil Katz, editor, *Contemporary Sociological Theory* (New York: Random House, 1971), p. 248.
14 The *Musselmaenner* walked around like zombies, entirely unreactive to their environment and, by this unresponsiveness, destined to die very soon. They had given up on life.
15 In the case of Primo Levi the route to suicide has been documented in a biography. See, Myriam Anissimor, *Primo Levi: Tragedy of an Optimist*. New York: The Overlook Press, 1999. She writes, "Forty years after his return (from Auschwitz) Levi was writing in torment about the

fact that he had survived when most of his comrades had died . . ." (p. 383); a few days before his death, in 1987, he telephoned the chief Rabbi of Rome, saying "I don't know how to go on. I can't stand this life any longer." (p. 405); two months before he had written to a friend that what he was now experiencing was worse than Auschwitz (p. 396). He had suffered from depression and had been on antidepressant medication. But, after a difficult recuperation from prostate surgery in March 1987, he had stopped taking the medication.

16 This chapter is couched in psychological terms. A different approach could concentrate on a society's culture patterns——and how these deal with dualisms. For example, the anthropologist Victor Turner spoke of rituals of status reversal: "The masking of the weak in aggressive strength and the concomitant masking of the strong in humility and passivity are devises that cleanse society of its structurally engendered 'sins'" *(The Ritual Process* [Chicago: Aldine, 1969], p. 185).

Moral Mutation—The Immediacy of Tomorrow?

The Great War—from 1914 to 1918—saw the massive use of what was, at the time, the most modern killing technology: tanks, poison gas, rapid-firing machine guns and long-range cannons. It also saw the relatively quick transportation of large armies so that they could be deployed in widely separated regions and still retain effectiveness. Above all, it saw trench warfare on an unprecedented scale.

In trench warfare, on any one day thousands upon thousands of men hacked each other to death. The individual soldier would climb out of his trench and, along with the comrades from his and adjacent trenches, storm toward the occupants of the opposing trench. If he did not manage to kill an opponent by rifle or machine gun fire at a distance, he rushed toward him and, with brute finality, plunged his bayonet into him. Then, if he himself was not too injured, he would advance onto the next enemy and repeat the process. This would continue until all were dead or so badly injured that they could not continue the scenario. The survivors would withdraw to their own trench, try to get replenishments, and renew the attack as soon as possible. Or, they would take turns to be defendants as the enemy enacted their own version of the attack scenario. This continued day after day, month after month, with virtually no change of territory. All took place on a scale that slaughtered a large portion of an entire generation of the young men of several countries.

Perhaps even more consequential than the actual horrifying killings was the moral mutation that went along with it—and which, to this day, remains incompletely understood and entirely unconfronted. I am speaking of the morality that enabled the young man to justify to himself that he was killing. He was killing total strangers. He was killing persons who, individually, were as innocent of wrongdoing as he was. He was killing people who, in terms of age and life experience, were at about the same stage as he was. He was killing men who had families who would be bereft and who would mourn their loved ones for the rest of their lives.

Contrary to what many think, these family members would never get over their lost loved one, who did not come back from the war or, if he did come back, might succumb to his wounds before long, to be remembered by an inscription in the family bible and, perhaps, by naming the next child after him. I am the bearer of such a name, that of my mother's brother, Emil.

How does the soldier justify his deeds? A simplistic explanation is that the enemy is seen as not a human being at all, that he is dehumanized. That therefore his death is not a human death. By killing him one is simply eliminating an inanimate obstacle. In World War II, the Gulf War and Kosovo War of the 1990s, with their great reliance on push-button technology and aerial bombings, this explanation might contain some truth. The individual soldier might never see the enemy he is killing. He might think of the enemy in abstract terms or, as happened in the Vietnam War, as meeting his quota of kills, with its focus on numbers.

This luxury of escape into abstraction did not apply in trench warfare. You saw the enemy into whom you plunged your bayonet. You saw his eyes. You heard his groans as he was dying after what you had done to him.

Perhaps. Perhaps, in the long-term emotional "shell shock" exhibited by many soldiers after World War I these soldiers kept on seeing the soldier they had killed. Perhaps soldiers suffering from "Gulf War Syndrome" symptoms remember the human side of the enemy during the Gulf War? Perhaps we see a stubborn subconscious revulsion against one's own participation in killing? Perhaps one's subconscious is asserting a moral accounting even while one's conscious actions try to ignore that morality. Perhaps the enemy was human—and you, his killer knew it.

Much of the effort to understand the emotional pain of soldiers—such as "shell shock" after World War I and the "psychic numbing" that showed up in veterans' hospitals after World War II and the Vietnam War – later popularized as Post Traumatic Stress Disease -- has assumed that the source of the pain was that soldiers saw horrors. They saw a buddy killed, right next to them. They saw horribly mutilated friends die painfully, and so forth. It seems to me, however, that a much deeper psychic wound might be due to soldiers realizing that they themselves had inflicted such horrors on other human beings. They themselves had done it, and there is a moral accounting.

Consciously, to justify their actions, soldiers do what all human beings do. They devise a moral justification. They do so because humans are moral creatures. We need moral justification for what we do––without it we cannot live with ourselves. And that moral justification almost invariably builds on our existing moral heritage; it does not suddenly spring an entirely new morality on us. Instead, it relies on repackaging our existing morality and, thereby, reformulating that existing morality so that it justifies to ourselves what we are now doing. Repackaging typically includes rearranging one's existing values, adopting different priorities among them, and assuring oneself that one's values are intact––even though one has made some wrenching changes.

Applying this reasoning to trench warfare, this means that the enemy soldier into whom you are about to plunge your bayonet is not dehumanized. Instead, you regard him as a terrible threat to all that is human, all that you regard as worthy and sacred, all for which you––and your country, your people, your heritage and you personally––stand. You persuade yourself––with serious help from your government––that by killing this enemy you are performing a profoundly moral deed. It is a deed that is in keeping with your moral heritage. Your life will be better. Even if you give your life to this cause, everyone for whom you care will be better because of your deed. In short, in its convoluted way, the enemy is humanized. He is humanized as the obstacle to everything that you regard as human. By eliminating him you are making a most "human" contribution. You have become a killer by moral necessity. In your own view, you remain a moral human being. The repackaging of your moral world has done its work.

For the title of this chapter I choose the concept "mutation" deliberately. The concept, as it is used in biology, carries the meaning that once a change has taken place––in the form of an aberration from what has existed in the past––it can become a permanent element of the repertoire of a species. Analogously, in human societies a mutation can become a permanent part of the repertoire of a culture, its configuration of "acceptable" behavior practices. It can become an ingredient to be used in the future. It can become part of the regular order within which communal life will henceforth take place. How does a cultural mutation that justifies mass killings develop? The first phase consists of regarding the initial killings as contributions that promote a high moral cause. This viewpoint becomes part of the cultural lore of what was a laudable––even sanctified––activity. The second phase consists of appealing to that initial series of sanctified mass killings to justify subsequent mass killings––again on supposedly high moral grounds This time completing the work begun in the first phase, of producing moral justification for mass killing.

In the case of the sanctified trench warfare killings, we see that it may have become a precedent[1] for morally justifying later mass killings, such as the killings in the millions that took place in World War II; killings where modern technology is amalgamated with direct, face-to-face killings; killings when, at the moment of battle, the enemy is regarded as totally beyond redemption––an obstacle to the very core of one's morality that must be eliminated.

From the Nazi German perspective in World War II, the Allied enemies were regarded as stubborn obstacles to Germany's moral destiny that must be eliminated if Germany's moral purity and destiny was to prevail. From the perspective of the Western Allies, Nazi Germany represented the ultimate moral degeneracy, which must be eliminated if the Western way of life–– the Western moral system––was to survive. Both sides remembered the deadly war of 1914-1918 and, rather than being shocked into impotence by the mass slaughter, were energized by that "supreme sacrifice" of life, suffered by one's own side, into entering into a second phase of that combat.

The most frightening product of World War I, then––even going beyond the actual horrors that were committed––is that a moral mutation may have been created that has thus far been accepted as part of our ongoing social order. What does it say about the immediacy of tomorrow? Will that mutation be the catalyst for more moral decay, for total moral misanthropy and decline––a morally disabling rider to our very existence? Or will we wake up and see to it that this mutation will not survive? Technically, can one amputate this mutation? Can one eliminate this particular piece of societal DNA? Thus far, this mutation has been frighteningly recalcitrant. It has been used to justify increasingly sophisticated techniques of mass killings and, at the same time, keep intact the "acceptability" of direct, face-to-face killings during military combat in the name of national honor and other noble causes

Some will argue that what I have been calling a mutation (of our moral order) is not some sort of sudden, Lamarckian change but instead is a gradually evolving––Darwinian––transformation that evolved long before World War I. Perhaps. But this does not change the apparent moral justification of killings––both technologized mass killings and personal, face-to-face killings––that seems to have taken up residence in our moral domicile. That residency makes claims on our tomorrows.

NOTE

1   Please note, I am saying that trench warfare may have become a precedent——not the *only* precedent——of the mass horrors of World War II.

Switchings:
Drastic Reconfigurations in Immediacy

After I arrived in America in 1947 I enrolled in a two-semester survey course on American history in night school at the City College of New York. The first semester ended with the Civil War. The second semester began with the Civil War. One semester was taught by a black instructor. One semester was taught by a white instructor. Both instructors covered the Civil War.

The American Civil War was portrayed differently by each of these instructors. The black instructor saw it as revolving entirely around the issue of slavery. The white instructor saw it as revolving entirely around economic issues. I, of course, was entirely confused.

With many years of hindsight, I now see that two totally different perspectives were brought to bear on the same phenomenon. Each was persuasive. Each was fully rounded and complete. Each was impervious to the other. In another section of this book I discuss the contributions of Gestalt psychology. At City College, it seems, we had a demonstration of Gestalt psychology applied to the Civil War. Each instructor brought to bear a distinctive point of view, resulting in an entire cognitive configuration––a gestalt––about the nature of the Civil War.

The City College experience also highlights a shortcoming in the work of the gestaltists. Yes, they demonstrate how a whole perspective is apt to be switched on and then color everything one sees. But it does not clarify how such a perspective may, itself, be comprised of diverse component parts that are, somehow, amalgamated into one package; and, once amalgamated, whether the seeds for drastic switching of perspective do not remain an option.

In another part of this book and in previous writings, I have emphasized that an individual may accept such a package *in toto* by becoming attached merely to one of its component parts. For example, during the Hitler era a German citizen may have joined the SS to find a job, not because of agreement with its genocidal programs. But having joined, that person would be very likely to become engaged in actually carrying out these programs, even though one did not believe in them. In practical terms, there could be acceptance of the entire Nazi package, even though there was personal commitment—initially, at least—to merely the economics of having a job. It turned out that such partially committed persons made significant contributions to the Nazi package, even to the components they resented. In short, the "amalgamation" consists of harvesting the contributions of people to a horrible cause, people who have only partial commitments to that cause while, dormantly, retaining entirely different commitments. These can be seeds for drastic switching of perspective.

On the one hand, we frequently see that a particular perspective is entirely impervious to different perspectives, to anything that calls its particular point of view into question. For example, during the 1930s many intellectuals—in the West as well as in the Soviet Union—saw great appeal in Soviet Communism. When confronted by information about Stalin's murderous campaigns against the Kulaks and others, this information was dismissed as mere capitalistic lies. It was ignored, even by highly intelligent people.

As I write these words, the second trial of O. J. Simpson has just been completed. In the first trial a mostly black jury found Simpson innocent of murdering his (white) wife and her (white) friend. In the second trial, a civil case, a largely white jury found Simpson "liable" for these two deaths. Following each trial, in the wider community blacks and whites were divided in their reactions to the trial. Blacks, by a large majority, judged the first trial's outcome fair and appropriate. Whites, by a large majority, judged the trial's outcome to be unfair and inappropriate. Following the second trial, views in the wider community again followed racial lines. Many blacks regarded the outcome to be unfair and inappropriate; many whites judged it to be fair and appropriate. It seems that each race had a distinctive perspective. Each was unable to hear the other side's perspective with any openness. Each was able to muster very persuasive arguments in favor of its particular point of view. One argument I heard made by blacks concerning the second trial, was that the white jury was simply "getting even" with blacks for their first verdict—as though this was a racial fight, not an issue of whether Simpson had actually committed murder. Whites, on the other hand, claimed that "race was not an issue."

The upshot is that distinctive perspectives can be firmly entrenched, and impervious to other points of view.

On the other hand, there are instances of perspectives undergoing full flip-flops—of adherents to a particular perspective suddenly and totally switching their allegiance to that perspective. Toward the end of the 1930s, for example, there took place a sudden and virtually total switch of allegiance by Father Coughlin's followers for his radio program. Over more than a decade Father Coughlin had built a vast following, using the public media as well as his pulpit to spread his message of populism and violent anti-Semitism. His followers had seemingly been fully committed to him and his message. Yet the arrival of World War II saw a dramatic departure of his followers. That departure was sudden and unexpected. The followers switched their allegiance quite abruptly. (I'll explain more fully in a moment.)

Another instance of sudden and drastic switching occurred toward the end of the civil rights movement in the late 1960s. That movement was geared to achieving political and social rights for American blacks. Martin Luther King Jr. was its leader. Among the ranks of those who participated alongside blacks were, relatively speaking, a large number of Jews.

At one stage in the movement's development some black leaders—not Dr. King—publicly embraced the Palestine Liberation Organization, then widely regarded as a terrorist movement bent on destroying the state of Israel. This greatly shocked the Jewish community. As a result, many Jews dropped out of active involvement in the civil rights movement. The switch was sudden and wrenchingly painful to these individuals, since they still believed in the objectives of the civil rights movement.

Both instances point to an anachronism in the persistence of perspectives toward the world: There can be unquestioning allegiance to a particular point of view, with seeming imperviousness to any contradicting points of view. And yet there can be drastic switching of allegiance, from one point of view to another point of view. How can this be? The gestaltists have not given us a formula for understanding the mechanism of switchings. I must confess my previous work on how an individual can be attached to a perspective—a package of values—by just one thread, also does not explain the process.

The answer, it seems, comes from the fact that when we are dealing with packages of values to which individuals are committed, some values can exist in a highly overt, publicly acknowledged state, whereas other values can exist and persist in an unacknowledged, dormant, recessive state. These latter values are occasionally fully activated, with drastic consequences.

In the case of Jewish participants in the civil rights movement, their social liberalism was highly visible and active. Their Jewish identity issues—what does it mean to be a Jew? what is the place of Israel in Jewish life?—were largely in a state of abeyance. These were not active issues to be confronted in their daily life. However, when the PLO issue arose, the Jewish participants in the civil rights movement were suddenly having to confront their "Jewish" identity values. These abruptly gained prominence and dominance in their ongoing perspective and actions. It entirely transformed their affiliation with a movement to which they had been committed on the grounds of their humane values which, they felt up to that time, did not affect their Jewish identity in any way. The intrusion of affiliation with the PLO changed all that. Their Jewish identity, and the perceived threat to the survival of Israel, did become an issue. As a result they went through a drastic reconfiguration of their perspective about the civil rights movement, and their own place in it. A new immediacy arose and prevailed.

In the case of the Father Coughlin movement there similarly was an activation of a largely dormant, recessive value. Namely, the matter of patriotism. In his public pronouncements and exhortations Coughlin had openly sided with Hitler's Germany and Benito Mussolini's Italy. While the United States was at peace and had diplomatic relations with these countries, it seemed to many of Coughlin's followers that it was entirely appropriate to sympathize with the accomplishments of Hitler and Mussolini, even to the point of accepting Hitler's anti-Semitism. But when it became clear that America was about to go to war with the two fascist countries, Coughlin's followers had to confront the fact that their loyalty to their country in time of war was becoming an issue. They chose loyalty to their country. It transformed their commitment, leading them away from Father Coughlin. They did so quite abruptly. Here, too, a new immediacy arose and prevailed.

Summarizing all this, there can be a sudden switch of a group's behavior commitments when a previously DORMANT commitment is ACTIVATED. The switch can be drastic – producing a group's total change of behavior – and entirely unexpected.

Can one make use of this insight to address the current ISIS phenomenon, the murderous mass movement operating largely in the Middle East but tending to spread to other parts of the globe? Specifically, what are some of its followers' dormant components? How might one activate these? At present the West's response to ISIS is entirely military – and not very successful. So, look at dormancies as a source of vulnerability might be helpful.

Fusions That Create a New Immediacy:
A *Look at Some Aspects of the Spanish Inquisition*

Let us turn to transformation in an entirely different era, location and scale of action, namely Spain in the years leading up to the Inquisition toward the end of the fifteenth century. There a new social order––a new social immediacy that claimed moral legitimacy––was envisioned. That new order aimed to drastically reduce the power of the king and his retinue of nobles and supplant them with another social class. Those opposed to the king deliberately created a rider, namely murderous anti-Semitism, and used it as the catalyst to create that new social order. Their eventual success illustrates the capacity of riders to transform a social order and influence the direction in which an entire nation's social order will go. This also illustrates that a rider––even if it advocates an extreme position––may gain moral respectability precisely because it has led to restructuring of the social order.

The following essay is based on the study by Benzion Netanyahu, 'The Origins of the Inquisition in Fifteenth Century Spain' *(New York: Random House, 1995). However, the concept of a rider is not used by Netanyahu. It is introduced here to augment his study by connecting it to the more general analysis of how social transformations can take place.*

Netanyahu (the father of Israel's current prime minister) disagrees with the view of many scholars that the Spanish Inquisition arose because the formerly converted Jews (conversos) were secretly still practicing Judaism, and that, as a consequence, the attack on these persons was primarily based on religious grounds.

Netanyahu proposes a new way of thinking about the persecution of the conversos. He claims that most of the conversos were full-fledged Christians who had practiced Christianity unreservedly for many years. They were fully assimilated into Christianity. Some had even achieved high office within the Church. Netanyahu gives a chilling reminder of how far their assimilation went: "In 1468, the Jews of Sepulveda were subjected to the torment of blood accusation [of killing Christ and, more recently, other Christians], and in 1471, eight of them were sentenced to death . . . The court responsible for that atrocious verdict was presided over by Juan Arias Davila, bishop of Segovia and himself a New Christian [a former Jew, a converso]" (p. 733).

The Inquisition, according to Netanyahu, was caused by a fusion of racism with a long, drawn-out power struggle that lasted over several decades. Anti-Semitism was deliberately used by the challengers to the existing power structure, headed by the king and the nobles - some of whom were conversos - who served him. The challengers used widely shared, but largely dormant anti-Semitism to recruit the Spanish population into their cause.

In short, Netanyahu's view is that fomented anti-Semitism was quite deliberately and calculatedly used by the agitators against the existing Spanish regime in order to rally support for their campaign against the existing political power structure they wanted to overthrow. Those making the attack on the conversos claimed that there was pollution of Spanish blood by these "Jews." But their real purpose, Netanyahu tells us, was that they expected to gain political power through the persecution of these people.

Netanyahu tells us that by the early 1400s the converses had become a highly privileged class, powerful and close to the king. Some served in high government office. They were resented by the lower classes and, most especially, by the upper classes who themselves wanted to wield power. The conversos were part of the power struggle and "besides the hostility toward the conversos that grew out of their involvement in the political conflict there was the old, deep-rooted hatred for Jewish converts which had always been felt by the Christians of Spain. That hatred formed the substratum of the hostility and, in addition, the breeding ground. In a sense, therefore, the *old* hatred was the *root* of the new ones" (p. 252-53).

By 1480, King Ferdinand––who personally had close and cordial relations with the conversos, one of whom was his own physician––finally acceded to the demands of his opponents and agreed to the beginnings of formal Inquisition proceedings against the conversos. After that there was no stopping the escalating process of persecution of the conversos and other Jews.

The following section accepts Netanyahu's analysis, but rephrases it in terms of the psychology of immediacy I am adopting in this book. I hope this will add not only to the power of Netanyahu's explanation of the Inquisition in particular, but to better understanding of how restructuring of a social order can come about. Specifically, I am pointing to the role of riders in guiding new fusions, new amalgams of values. In the case of the Inquisition, this process created opportunity to persecute new "enemies," pry open the existing social order and legitimize highly costly ventures. Not the least of the lessons from all this may be that a high degree of assimilation may create a new kind of vulnerability for the "assimilated" category of persons. It is precisely their success in gaining access to power plus the lingering shadow of their distant past that may create their vulnerability to being used for creating new fusions, new social amalgams of social power, through which they may, once again, become the primary victims.

The Inquisition was built on desiring a new immediacy, a new social and political "reality" for Spain of the late fifteenth century. It utilized existing tensions and power struggles, but injected into them deliberately activated dormant themes of suspicion and hatred of conversos. It forged these newly activated themes into a catalytic rider that would foster the restructuring of Spain's social order. It would threaten to bring down the king and his retinue of nobles or, at least, force him to listen to an entirely different cast of actors on Spain's national scene. It would create a new political amalgam.

That new amalgam, under stimulation from the loudly proclaimed rider, became increasingly compelling. According to Netanyahu, the new amalgam was not based on one sudden act but instead took some decades to nurture and develop. It seems that each failed attempt to provoke anti-Semitic action against the conversos––which took place over a number of decades––ended with some added increment of suspicion, bordering on hatred, being placed in silent storage within the cultural heritage of Spain. It would remain there, waiting to be fed when the next failed installment of action against the converses arrived and help it grow even more. Once the dormant anti-Semitism erupted successfully and became the dominant political pattern for the entire country, it became a model of what was going to happen in Nazi Germany some 400-plus years later. Here was an amalgamation process that, thanks to the explicit and persistent use of anti-Semitism as a rider, gained increasing momentum and public legitimacy.

The new amalgam eventually achieved a life of its own, overcoming all opposition. The former acceptance of many of the conversos as well-respected citizens was now undermined. Highly esteemed individuals were suddenly treated as criminals and pariahs. The new political amalgam became a zealously adhered-to Local Moral Universe, with its own moral imperatives that accepted no compromises or deviations from its crusading course.

An unanswered question remains: What conditions favor emergence of uncompromising, Local Moral Universes––such as the Inquisition, the one described by Netanyahu? Or, as Nazi Germany's? The use of one particular rider––such as activating dormant anti-Semitism––is not an adequate explanation of why that particular rider succeeds in rallying people to accept a restructuring of their existing social reality.

I am convinced that it is not the particular rider, such as anti-Semitism, but the *manner of use* of the rider which is crucial. For instance, the fact that a new amalgam is portrayed as a restructuring of the existing social order––rather than a totally newly invented social order––can be very persuasive and beguiling. So can the activation of dormancies––dormant prejudices, fears, superstitions. It, too, can aid the assumption that the new social movement is really making use of long-existing social commitments. It claims, merely, to be revitalizing them, resulting in a new order that is fresh, vibrant, and valid. The rider is used to justify the "need" for the restructuring of the society, and show that the new order connects the present with meaningful historic experiences and, supposedly, highlighting basic existing values and, indeed, augmenting these old values.

In Nazi Germany, the initial master rider––for justifying the Nazi brand of restructuring the priorities of the German people after World War I––was the theme that Germans must wash away the shame suffered at the hands of the powers that prevailed against it in World War I. Hitler would be the leader to accomplish this sacred and morally compelling crusade. To be sure, anti-Semitism was included in the earliest formulation of the Nazi credo. But it was only later, after the Nazis gained power, that *it* became the master rider, the core theme, that was used to hold together the Nazi coalition of interest groups, the amalgam we know as Nazism. Here, anti-Semitism––the supposed Jewish threat to the very existence of Germany and its profound destiny––became the rider that was a *perpetuation* catalyst for Nazism, whereas the early theme of washing away the German shame had been the rider that served as the primary *generative* catalyst.

Here, then, is an explanation of the furious continuation of the Nazi program of genocide of the Jews. It would perpetuate the entire Nazi amalgam, most especially its mythical dimension of fostering the purity of the Nordic-German race. By focusing on the genocidal crusade it gave Nazism a "moral" mission, directing a march toward a mythical heroic eternity. Even while its current military ventures were beginning to fail it would still come awesomely close to accomplishing its mythical moral mission by exterminating the Jewish people. That pursuit, in its own right, would elevate the Nazi cause to Wagnerian dimensions of moral grandeur and eternity, where one military defeat was but a brief interruption on the road to ultimate victory.

In the case of the Inquisition, it is not clear whether there were separate "generative" and "perpetuating" riders. It seems that the persecution of conversos and Jews gained a great deal of momentum at some point, and after that it could no longer be challenged, even though it proved to be economically expensive and disruptive for Spain to keep on displacing the conversos and Jews–– just as it became expensive and disruptive for Germans to continue the persecution of Jews to lethal extremes, using scarce resources when these might have helped the German war effort. The persecutions––in Spain just as, later, in Germany––became more than a rider. They became an end in themselves.

How do generative riders emerge? One virtually saw a generative rider suddenly emerge over the 'Bitburg Affair'. It happened in response to President Ronald Reagan's planned trip to Germany. This was during the West's Cold War against the Soviet Union. The trip was intended to recruit Germany into the West's camp. It was to include having the president visit the German military cemetery at Bitburg. When it became known that this cemetery was the resting place of notorious SS men and soldiers who had fought against American soldiers, American veterans and Jews were outraged. They joined forces in publicly opposing the president's visit to the Bitburg cemetery. They succeeded in getting the American government to change its plans for the Reagan visit.

Here was a particular event—the president's proposed visit to the German military cemetery—that became a generative rider to briefly fuse very diverse social forces – namely Veterans Associations and Jewish Associations. These forces, in turn, demanded—and achieved—some fundamental changes in American policy. It all began fortuitously, quickly and without plan.

By contrast, the generative rider of the Inquisition—symbolized by the Jew as enemy—was not a fortuitous, quick affair. It was deliberately nurtured over a period of decades, overcoming a number of setbacks before it prevailed. It was planted and utilized quite deliberately, making use of long-simmering anti-Semitism to create a new fusion, a new political reality, a new power alignment wherein the king ceded much power to his adversaries. In that new fusion—that new immediacy—the conversos were the symbolic rider, the supreme enemy, standing for a power structure that supposedly ought to be overthrown.

The conversos, the Jews who were so seemingly assimilated into Christian society, turned out to be most vulnerable precisely because of their assimilation into the larger society. Those who wanted to transform that society picked on them as suitable instruments to accomplish their sedition. They saw in the conversos members of the society who had reached high and powerful status while still retaining faint tinges of outsiderness. These tinges were used to foster doubt, not only about the conversos themselves but about the entire existing social order—notably the king and his retinue—that had permitted this to happen while at the same time leaving entire segments of the society in a state of discontent. It seems that the conversos were ideal fodder to foment discontent for the entire system. Stated differently, the conversos were vulnerable because dormant anti-Semitism could be activated and turned against them. In turn, the attack on the conversos—given their privileged position—could be used to pry open the existing social order.

In the end both sides of the conflict saw it in their interest to sacrifice the conversos. The alienated outsiders did so deliberately, at the outset of the struggle, in order to gain power——using hatred and persecution of conversos as the rider to bring a new social order into existence. The entrenched royalty did so, eventually and reluctantly, to try to retain power——using hatred and persecution of conversos as a rider that would fuse the existing social order into a new shape, one that could stave off the attack on it.

In the Inquisition, and at Bitburg, a new immediacy came into existence. It was the result of a rider guiding a process of transformation which, then, gained impetus, giving the rider a life of its own. The source of such a rider——be it from the deliberate nurturing of long dormant perceptions and prejudices (in the case of the Inquisition) or from the sudden and fortuitously coalescing interest groups (as in the Bitburg Affair)——is not the issue. The issue is the fact that a new fusion——a new amalgam of social forces——has come into existence (briefly, in the case of Bitburg and sustainedly in the case of the Inquisition). It now claims moral legitimacy for its program of action and for the rider that guides it. That rider, whatever its source, and no matter how crazy and extreme it may have seemed when it first arrived on the scene, may gain total dominance over the course of action once the fusion has taken place, creating an entirely new immediacy, a new social order, and a new moral legitimacy for the rider itself.

Perhaps the major lesson is the final dominance of a particular rider. The rider first served as catalyst for developing a new fusion of social forces. From that fusion it gained ultimate moral respectability for its message. Here, indeed, is a self-fulfilling prophecy.

A disconcerting lesson, surely, is that assimilation——the effort of a particular category of people to become fully incorporated into the cultural mainstream of the society in which they live——can create a unique form of vulnerability for these people. It can be a by-product of their conspicuous participation in the mainstream. Their vulnerability exists as long as minor antipathies and prejudices, or possibly outright hatred toward them continue in dormant form——and are available for future activation.

Fred Emil Katz

In the Spanish case, it meant activating dormant anti-Semitism in order to undermine the existing power structure. Since there were Jews in prominent positions in the existing power structure, that power structure was deemed vulnerable to attack by those who wanted to gain power. All they needed to do – and did do – was to use anti-Semitism to produce cracks in the existing power structure.

In the Nazi German case, it meant activating dormant anti-Semitism in order to harness support for pursuing Hitler's dream of Germany's racial purity and national grandeur. Since, in the Nazi view, Jews were a separate 'race' – an inferior and most dangerous one at that – their very existence and prominence in virtually every field of human endeavor, was deemed to undermine Germany's grand destiny. They stood in the way. If Jews were eliminated then Germany's grandeur was well on its way to becoming a reality.

In both cases, a subgroup's prominent participation in the larger society proved to be as dubious blessing.

The Unknowable in Immediacy:
Introduction to the Location of Local Autonomy

The previous sections explored four dimensions of the immediate world in which we live. We can identify these dimensions. We can "know" them. Now I shall point to a different sort of dimension. It is about the very nature of knowing. Here is a proposition I shall have us consider: Some form of unpredictability——I am calling it *bounded indeterminacy*——is itself a form of orderliness in the immediate world in which we live. Within many, perhaps most, systems of human interaction there exist distinct and identifiable areas of behavior where individual acts cannot be predicted. There are limits to knowing. This need not be a bad thing. Indeed it may be useful and necessary that in some systems of human behavior locally initiated discretionary behavior be allowed to exist. When this operates within defined boundaries we know what we cannot predict, what we cannot know. We may know this quite precisely. That is, we may know precisely the limits of not knowing. Knowing these limits can contribute to the functioning of social systems. It can contribute flexibility and viability.

The following essay on bounded indeterminacy was prepared for an audience of physicists. It was written in the 1970s while I was teaching sociology at Tel Aviv University. At the time Jewish physicists (and other Jewish scientists) in the Soviet Union were not allowed to attend international scientific conferences. In response it was decided to hold an international physics conference in Moscow, so that the Soviet Jewish scientists might have access to their international colleagues. It was also decided to widen the participation in the proposed conference to include scientists from other fields. Papers were solicited. I was going to be one of the participants; I prepared the bounded indeterminacy paper for the conference.

To no one's great surprise we were refused permission to hold the conference. However, our effort drew attention to the plight of the Soviet Jewish scientists. The papers were assembled and published in the form of a book.[1]

My essay has some affinity with––but also some crucial differences from––two significant scientific formulations developed during the twentieth century: Werner Heisenberg's Uncertainty Principle and Kurt Goedel's proof of certain limitations of mathematics.

NOTE

1   Norman A. Chigier and Edward A. Stern, editors, *Collective Phenomena and the Application of Physics to Other Fields of Science* (Fayetteville, NY: Brain Research Publications, 1975).

Fred Emil Katz

Immediacy and Not-Knowing:
The Case of Bounded Indeterminacy: An Essay in Systems Theory[1]

I. Background

Many systems found in the actual world––be they those made by humans or naturally occurring ones––do not seem to be completely determinate. This fact has attracted attention of many scientists, from stochastic model builders (notably Markovians who create increasingly precise mathematical ways of estimating outcomes of a series of system states when each state is influenced by chance factors) to General System theorists (notably Ludwig von Bertalanffy, who introduced the conception of open-systems to stand alongside closed, i.e., fully determinate systems), to physicists (notably Heisenberg and his Uncertainty Principle), to Goedel and his proof of the unprovability of certain mathematical axioms, to engineers who include "play" or "tolerance" for some variability in the design of machines. In a philosophical sense all of these approaches recognize limitations to what is scientifically knowable. Explicitly or implicitly they all suggest ways of living with the fact that indeterminacy exists. Importantly: they all try to reduce its impact.

The objective of my discussion is not to offer yet another scheme for minimizing the effects of indeterminacy. Rather, the objective is to show that a certain form of indeterminacy is a useful and necessary component part of at least some systems. The emphasis will be on indeterminacy being a system-based phenomenon in its own right. The discussion rests on the proposition that indeterminacy needs to be, and can be, explicitly incorporated into theories that describe the structure and functioning of systems. It does it by proposing that there exists a phenomenon of bounded indeterminacy within many systems. The boundedness––i.e., the limits within which there exists indeterminacy––can be specified precisely, while at the same time accepting the unspecifiablity of what lies within these limits.

It may seem that the previously mentioned approaches already fully explain indeterminacy that influences scientific work with systems. It may seem, for instance, that stochastic models already resolve the matter of indeterminacy; that they do, in fact, measure the amount of uncertainty that exists in a particular system when they indicate the probability of particular occurrences, and that the Markovians adequately deal with it when sequences, or chains, of probable occurrences are at issue.

It must be recognized that when stochastic models concern themselves with uncertainty their objective is to reduce uncertainty as much as possible by producing estimates of probable future system-states. The thrust of the procedure is to reduce indeterminacy as much as possible. They do so with the objective of extracting some measure of certainty from within the range of uncertainty. It is as though uncertainty were a field of waste matter from which one wants to extract some usable matter. This approach does not credit indeterminacy with being potentially useful to systems.

To begin to illustrate the usefulness of indeterminacy let us note a query by the cyberneticist Ross Ashby. He asked if a man has but ten minutes to teach his son a new language, should he use the time to teach him as many words as possible or should he use the time to teach him the use of a dictionary? Obviously the latter offers far greater potential for learning the language than does the former. But equally obviously the dictionary way is a far less determinate approach. Perhaps the son will not actually use the dictionary and, therefore, will not learn any words at all; but on the other hand, he may learn a vast number of words, far more than he could possibly have learned from his father in ten minutes. The indeterminacy of learning from the dictionary points to vastly increased options in the process of learning. To be sure the options may be used for non-learning; the son may never open the dictionary. But the options may also be used for a great deal of learning. In short, the indeterminate character of the teaching process here incorporates some negative but also some very definite positive potentials for the learning process.

I propose to explore positive uses of indeterminacy in systems. The objective is not to enter into the tired old philosophical debate on the nature of determinism. The objective is not, even, to redirect philosophical thinking about determinism, although this could be a welcome by-product. The objective is to point to more effective research on systems by suggesting some changes in systems theory. But first let me briefly review some precursors to the present approach a bit more.

In physics, engineering and mathematics one can discern the rudiments of a perspective that accommodates itself to a degree of persisting indeterminacy among orderly, stable structures. In physical systems one finds acceptance of a kind of indeterminacy in subatomic levels of activity. The Heisenberg Uncertainty Principle suggests that at the subatomic level measurement techniques will themselves interfere with the things being measured. It is not a matter of defective measurement procedures. It is a matter inherent to the character of subatomic particle systems: Some ways of measuring them must be used, but the measurement procedure will inevitably influence what is being measured. Hence one must accept a degree of uncertainty as to the exact activity of the individual particles. But this is not fatal since, for many purposes, probability mathematics––based on gross number of occurrences––enables one to calculate the activity of particles with sufficient precision. Here, then, is a way to cope with the unknowable at the micro-level by addressing it at a macro-level.

In the Heisenberg formulation one assumes that the actual subatomic physical systems are determinate. It is merely a matter of not being able to devise measurement strategies that can describe the activity of individual particles. But this is a questionable assumption. What is certainly known is that we do not know (and cannot know) the precise activities of the individual particles. It does not follow that the activities of these individual particles, in a system of interacting particles, is determinate. Or, stated differently, by describing the activity of the particles in a gross manner–– because this can be done by probability mathematics––one claims to describe a system of activity of individual particles. This is postulating something about one system while describing another.

However, for present purposes, the most important point is that Heisenberg found a way of accepting and coping with a sector of unknowability. For all practical purposes that sector is indeterminate as far as the human "knower" is concerned. This represents the point of view that scientific precision can be preserved even under conditions of uncertainty.

A slightly different perspective toward indeterminacy exists for human-made physical systems, such as a machine, where one finds deliberate built-in "tolerance" patterns that imply acceptance of a degree of imprecision in actual systems. The degree of acceptable imprecision is likely to depend on cost considerations, on the state of technology, and on the task the machine is expected to perform. At any rate a degree of imprecision––or indeterminacy––is frequently acceptable. Indeed, it can be entirely necessary.

For instance, a wheel that rotates vertically on a horizontally placed shaft is usually allowed some small amount of horizontal motion by not regulating its place of rotation on the shaft with infinite precision. This allows for lubrication to be introduced and distributed by the sideways motion of the wheel. It also allows the wheel to "adapt" to the presence of particles of dust or other minor obstacles: it can move the particles aside or it can avoid them by moving away from them. If the wheel's place of rotation were fixed with utmost precision––if there were not some indeterminacy in the location of the wheel––then the wheel (and the rest of the machine) would break down each time some particles of dust appeared on the shaft where the wheel rotates. Obviously, however, the wheel cannot have unlimited horizontal movement if it is to remain articulated with the other parts of the machine. Typically one finds collars on the shaft on each side of the wheel that prevent the wheel from moving horizontally beyond specific points. The limits of the horizontal movement of the wheel are thereby controlled rigidly and precisely.

The main point that emerges from the preceding discussion, especially in relation to human-made machines, is that the limits of imprecision that a system can tolerate are related to the character of the total system. In the case of human-made systems these limits are often stated explicitly, as in the foregoing example of the wheel within a machine; beyond a certain level of "tolerance" the machine cannot absorb the wheel's indeterminate sideway motion on the shaft. This is likely to have been incorporated in the engineer's design of the machine. It is also likely to have been stated explicitly in the engineer's instructions to the manufacturer of the machine.

A corollary to the presence of indeterminacy in empirical systems is the fact that mathematics, probably the most determinate of analytic systems, also contains indeterminacy. Goedel's famous proof that some axioms of mathematics are unprovable constitutes an elegant example. He demonstrated that "it is impossible to establish the internal logical consistency of a very large class of deductive systems––elementary arithmetic, for example––unless one adopts principles of reasoning so complex that their internal consistency is as open to doubt as that of the systems themselves."[2] Goedel showed the obstinate and irreducible presence of indeterminacy within mathematical systems. Such indeterminacy appears to contradict the fully determinate nature of mathematics. Yet the rest of mathematics does not seem to be undermined by the indeterminacy demonstrated by Goedel.

Perhaps Goedel's proof concerning the indeterminacy in some segments of mathematics and Heisenberg's Uncertainty Principle concerning small-scale physical systems are an indication of what is a more general phenomenon. Namely that *for each system that exists in nature—and for each structural component of systems—there exist specifiable forms of indeterminacy.* By "specifiable" I mean that their precise location—their place within a system and their limits—are knowable. It is important to note that the forms of indeterminacy being proposed here are themselves structural properties of systems. That is the guiding thesis of this discussion. Stated differently, the guiding thesis is: Some forms of indeterminacy—of unknowability—are an essential feature of natural systems. Indeterminacy is here thought to be neither the randomly unknown nor the not-yet-known. It is the unknown that is locatable and specifiable within systems. It exists *within* the boundaries of systems.

This line of thinking will be supported from a consideration of social structures and social systems. The reason for turning to *social* structures and *social* systems is not that social systems demonstrate the presence of indeterminacy better than do other systems; nor is it that the presence of indeterminacy in social systems has been well recognized in the scientific literature; nor, emphatically, that indeterminacy is present in greater or lesser abundance in social systems than in other systems. I turn to social systems simply because, professionally, this is my home base. I am a social scientist. I know social systems better than other systems.

II. Indeterminacy in Social Systems

It will be shown that indeterminate behavior is incorporated in the very structure of social systems, be they large or small.

The smallest units of social structure are *roles*. Roles are structured within social systems in two ways. They contain specified and distinct packages of socially enforceable behavior, and they are linked to other roles, making up role systems.

1. Concerning enforceable behavior: Roles are "packages" of expected behavior. The teacher role, for example, contains the expected behavior of treating students fairly, having command of a body of knowledge, and presenting the teaching material in an orderly manner. These expectations are known not only to teachers but to students, school officials, and parents. This means that the expectations are indentifiable and enforceable. Stated slightly differently, the role's expected behavior content is "structured" in the sense that the expectations are known by the people with whom the teacher has dealings. These people can create enforcement of the expected behavior.

2. Concerning roles being linked to other roles: The role of teacher is in close interaction with the role of student, school principal, and parents. There can be no role of teacher without a role of student. The teacher role exists in complementary relation to the student role. Thus, for example, some of the "rights" in the teacher role (that students heed the teacher, that students do their assigned homework) are, at the same time, "duties" in the student role. Similarly one can speak of complementary relations between the engineer and client of that engineer, between the salesperson and customer of that salesperson, and finally, between the physician and patient of that physician.

Indeterminacy exists in all these relationships. Let me illustrate it from some component parts of the physician-patient relationship. The following sketch is not intended to be a complete description of that relationship.

When treating a patient the (Western) physician is expected to use objective scientific knowledge, whenever it is available; to refrain from personal emotional involvement with the patient––personal likes or dislikes are to be excluded, even when the physician does not approve of the patient's morality; not to take advantage of the patient, either financially or emotionally. Similarly, there are expectations that apply to the role of patient: As patient, one is expected to obey the physician; one is expected to withhold no information that is relevant to one's illness.

It will be obvious that the roles of physician and patient complement one another; that the physician's disinterested use of objective knowledge is augmented by the patient's trusting obedience of the physician's instructions.

It will also be obvious that the *expectations* do not fully describe what is actually taking place when physician and patient interact with one another.

(a)   The expectations are not complete. For instance, the expectations may not mention the patient's degree of anxiety while one carries out the physician's orders; they also may not mention how willingly and how carefully one carries out the instructions.

(b)   Even when the expectations do cover specific issues in the physician-patient relationship, they do not specify the precise actions that take place. The expectations do not state what the *specific* physician in a *specific* situation actually does. Is the physician jovial and outgoing or quiet and reserved? Is the physician efficient or hopelessly disorganized? None of these questions—and many more—are answered by the expected-behavior components of the physician role.

The expectations encompass behaviors that are generally believed to be legitimate as *long as they do not transcend the limits* that are incorporated in the expectations. When dispassionate efficiency becomes brutality, the limits have been transcended. When joviality becomes irresponsibility, the limits have been transcended. In each case the physician's behavior is regarded as illegitimate—and the entire system of trust between medical personnel and patients is thereby endangered.

In more abstract terms, the expectations are statements of limitations within which behavior must fall. The expectations typically have some tangible and sensible relation to the fundamental task at hand. In the case of the physician-patient situation, they are geared to relatively orderly deployment of medical knowledge in the service of healing sick people. (This does not mean that the expectations were deliberately designed with this in mind. They may have evolved accidentally or by trial and error over a period of time.) The physician can, through one's flexibility, adapt oneself to the particular patient and the particular immediate circumstances in which the physician and patient find themselves. Since medicine is a long way from being an exact science, this room to maneuver is absolutely essential. Hence a degree of indeterminacy that allows the physician some flexibility has very practical significance.

It must be reiterated that when we speak of *expectations* we are describing the *structure* of social systems. Thus if I, as a patient, know what to expect from my physician––that the physician not take advantage of me, that the physician use objective knowledge ––I know that there are limits to the physician's indeterminate behavior. I grant the physician a degree of discretion in making judgments about my illness––and this implies that I cannot fully predict the physician's behavior: It contains indeterminacy as far as I am concerned. I also know that if the physician crosses the boundary between legitimate and illegitimate discretion ––if the physician does try to take advantage of me––I may have the physician punished. All this means that the limits of indeterminate behavior in the role of physician are known and can be enforced. In short, they are socially structured. They are incorporated within the social system of the relationship between physician and patient; they are enforceable, if transcended, by legal mechanisms that exist in the larger social system.

It would be valuable to develop theorems about the optimal balance between indeterminacy in interactant roles. For example:

(1) Where one role involves bringing to bear specialized knowledge (by the physician, by the engineer, by the teacher) and the other role involves the role of dependent consumer of that knowledge (the patient, the client, the student).

   (a) How much indeterminacy can be incorporated in the dominant role before it becomes self-defeating or before the consumer loses confidence?

   (b) How much indeterminacy is necessary in the subordinate role? A complete automaton is not a good patient, presumably some discretionary indeterminacy is necessary even in the dependent role.

(2) Are there optimal indeterminacy ratios between unequal roles per se? If the roles are drastically unequal in terms of any resources––say, in their access to economic resources, or to affective-emotional resources, or to knowledge resources––are

there optimal proportions of indeterminacy for each role so that the unequal roles can interact effectively?

I have mentioned amounts of indeterminacy. But the effectiveness of indeterminacy may also be a matter of location: Where——in which sorts of behavior——does indeterminacy exist? Hence, a research question is:

(3)   Where, in the relation between unequal roles, must there be indeterminacy?

Small-scale social phenomena involve not only single roles. They also involve the life of groups. Sociologists and psychologists have devoted much energy to the study of small groups——both naturally occurring groups and artificially created groups in laboratory situations. Perhaps the most basic thing one finds in such groups is that each member is assigned a position within the group. Leaders may emerge and followers may emerge; pranksters may emerge; conflict-resolvers may emerge; and many more. Also, and dear to the heart of sociologists, ranking systems tend to emerge: Some members are regarded more highly than others.

The one ubiquitous fact is that people in groups are not left free-floating. They are assigned a "status," a position within the group. An interpretation of this fact is that a person's "position" in a group defines how one fits into the group. Stated more accurately, a person's position identifies and delineates one's participation in the group. Thus, the highly regarded member participates differently from the poorly regarded member; the leader is expected to lead; the prankster is expected to be amusing. But, in addition, each person's behavior is interpreted within the context of one's position: when the prankster speaks seriously, this is different from serious speech by the leader, who may be habitually serious. A position is a context——a cognitive gestalt——in terms of which behavior is judged.

A crucial fact is that here, just as in the case of roles, one does not know which precise acts of behavior will be forthcoming. Will the prankster pretend to break furniture or tell amusing stories? Will the leader suggest an attack on a rival group or propose making peace with that group? What is known is the rubric of behavior *within* which each individual is said to participate in the group. The precise item of behavior is not predetermined by the position; it is indeterminate. But the limits within which the indeterminate behavior falls are known; they are specified by the label that attaches to the position. Thus, let me repeat, the "leader" is expected to lead; precisely how one will lead is not usually spelled out in the position of leader.

In short, positions are contexts for participating in a social situation. These contexts permit some indeterminate behavior but, at the same time, they specify limits to indeterminate behavior: The prankster is not expected to be a leader, and the leader is not expected to be a prankster. A twofold theme emerges:

(1) For a given position there exists a given sphere of socially approved indeterminate behavior: The leader can innovate in the realm of leadership; the prankster can innovate in the realm of practical joking.

(2) Yet outside one's position indeterminate behavior is sharply curtailed. The prankster is not allowed to innovate leadership. To be sure, in his jokes the prankster may *suggest* new forms of leadership, but the prankster is not "in a position" to carry them out. The leader, on the other hand, cannot expect to engage in much practical joking and expect to retain "serious" obedience as leader.

In a sense the existence of social positions in a group constitutes a series of behavior reservoirs, each position being a separate reservoir from which behavior options are chosen. The specific options that will be chosen are not predetermined. But the limits within which the options fall are indeed known, since they are chosen from a specific reservoir. The reservoirs have labels attached to them, which are known to the members of the group. The group members enforce the use of behavior items by each occupant of a position from one of these, and only one of these, reservoirs.

Next, a brief look at one example of indeterminacy in large-scale social systems. Here, also, the "structuring" of indeterminacy follows distinct patterns.

The case of co-optation: A particular organization may be faced with external enemies. For instance, a government agency may encounter hostility from businesses in the community in which the agency operates. One way of meeting such opposition is for the threatened agency to co-opt part of its hostile environment. It may do so by appointing some of the hostile business leaders as consultants or as part-time officials in the agency. Such co-optation is apt to result in diminished hostility toward the agency. This is because the "enemies" are no longer completely free outsiders: they have become "insiders" who must play by the rules of the agency; their wings have been clipped. Yet they now have a chance to influence the agency from within.

In terms of indeterminacy, the co-opted persons reduce the indeterminacy facing the agency from the outside. The agency, by taking in the members of the opposition, has established communication with the outside world that is likely to result in fewer unpleasant surprises from the outside. The outside world becomes less indeterminate. And by incorporating leaders of the opposition it may transform hostile opposition into "loyal" opposition. It is apt to be more tame than the previous kind of opposition.

There is a price attached to the co-optation process. The alien outsiders who have been incorporated into the agency are apt to retain some of their enmity toward the agency and keep it alive within the agency. They are apt to spring surprises from within the organization, in the form of indeterminate behavior.[3] Criticism-from-within is likely to increase (in indeterminate ways). Yet oblivion to the outside is likely to decrease, resulting in more determinate behavior toward the environment by the agency's staff. These are important consequences resulting from the redistribution of indeterminacy.

In conclusion, *structuring* of indeterminacy points the way to regarding certain forms of indeterminacy——namely indeterminacy that exists in specified, limited areas——as component parts of social systems. The boundedness of such indeterminacy protects the system from dissolving into a state of utter unstructuredness. Usually when thinking of indeterminacy one thinks of it as being unbounded and therefore destructive to the operation of systems. On the contrary, I hope I have shown that there also exist forms of indeterminacy that are indeed structured within systems. They can be regarded as part of the persistent and necessary character of systems. They can enable a system to exist, to function effectively, to survive. The secret of such system-related indeterminacies is that the *limits*––the boundaries––of the indeterminacies are known. This enables systems to accept them, to utilize them, to benefit from them.

Concerning limits: The mathematical differential calculus is essentially a theory of limits. It focuses on ever-diminishing limits (and a method of calculating the consequences of these ever-diminishing limits). By contrast I am here suggesting a theory of the fixity of limits, where the fixity of limits bestows functional benefits on the existing structures in a system. It does so by specifying zones of local autonomy by component parts of the system. One might then state that $A = f(L)$ ––that the autonomy (A) of the component parts of a system is a function of the limits (L) within which they exist.

Perhaps this calls for a calculus of limit-fixity. One might calculate how the fixity of limits produces identifiable and measurable benefits for the structures whose activities it is both identifying and limiting. The limits specify where––in which zone of activity––indeterminate, locally autonomous activity takes place; and they specify how much such locally autonomous, indeterminate activity can take place while, at the same time, guaranteeing that it is not controlled by the rest of the system––that "within limits" it is, indeed, indeterminate–– although operating from within distinctive, system-contained launching points.

I have also suggested that structured indeterminacy can itself be traded––between a system and its environment––as in the case of cooptation. There, in return for accepting some additional "internal" indeterminacy, a system may reduce assaults on itself from "external" indeterminacy. Another example would be a psychotic patient being allowed to engage in a far greater range of indeterminate hallucinatory behavior while confined in a psychiatric facility than would be permitted "on the outside," while living among so-called normal people. Here, too, the location of indeterminate activity is being traded.

In both cases the location of indeterminate activity is crucial. Within the government agency, a measure of loyalty to the organization colors all activities, even the indeterminate ones. Hence, in trading external for internal indeterminacy, the organization has a net benefit––it has increased its chances of successful survival––since its loyalty-to-the-organization rider is likely to prevail over a wider range of activities. In the case of the management of a psychotic patient, too, there is net benefit: The psychiatric facility achieves it through a prevailing rider over the patient's activities––in the form of the right to physically restrain the patient in return for the patient's right to engage in wildly hallucinatory behavior, none of which would be permitted on the outside. In each case the trading of indeterminacy means a change of location where a zone of indeterminate activity can take place. It also means that each location imposes its own riders on that indeterminate activity, coloring it even while permitting a range of indeterminate activity to exist. In both cases, we are seeing an economy based on an exchange of pieces of structured indeterminacy. The indeterminacies are nurtured by social contexts and these, in turn, exercise a measure of influence over the indeterminate activity through their own pervasive riders while, at the same time, permitting the indeterminacies to exist.

The inspiration for this chapter has been that when we look at systems––social systems in particular––we must acknowledge that we often have incomplete knowledge of how things work. Much of science is devoted to diminishing this incomplete knowledge, under the assumption that entirely complete knowledge is possible and, ideally, necessary if we are to understand how systems actually operate. By contrast, this chapter has suggested that some forms of incomplete knowledge––what I have called bounded indeterminacy––are actually a necessary component of systems. They need to be incorporated into our scientific models of systems, at least into the models of social systems.

Stated differently, the chapter suggests that indeterminacy represents a form of local autonomy among some (perhaps most) component parts of systems. And most important, the precise location of such local autonomy––the zone in which it exists––can often be identified. This makes it possible to have viable models of systems and their functioning that includes both precisely defined component parts as well as local discretionary behavior by these component parts. The conjoint workings of both can produce more realistic scientific models of the actual character of systems.[4]

NOTE

1 Previous versions of this chapter were published in *Behavioral Science* (19, no. 6, November 1974) and in *Collective Phenomena and the Application of Physics to Other Fields* (Norman A. Chigier and Edward Stern, editors, Fayetteville, NY: Brain Research Publications, 1975)

2 Ernest Nagel and James R. Newman, *Goedel's Proof*, New York: New York University Press, 1960, p. 6.

3 An extreme version of such reverse co-optation was the election of Ronald Reagan––who regarded government as the enemy of the people––as head of the American government.

4 Persons familiar with the work of Alfred North Whitehead will recognize my indebtedness to his "organismic" approach to science. See his *Science and the Modern World* (New York: Mentor Books, 1956). Whitehead's work is focused largely on the world of the physical sciences. It is an outcome of his own professional career as a mathematician who, late in life, turned to a career in philosophy.

Conclusion

This book began with the statement that from the moment of our birth every single one of us must cope with the world around oneself. The book demonstrated that our coping behaviors are not random flailing. They contain distinct patterns of orderliness. Five of these were explored. Together, they form an emerging paradigm for understanding IMMEDIACY.

We cannot dismiss immediacy as merely ephemeral events and, therefore, neither worth studying nor capable of being studied systemically. On the contrary, I hope the emerging paradigm points to a glimmer of real gold that is ready to be mined. As is the case with any paradigm, this one contains new, unanswered questions––such as, at which point does an impinging rider change from being a catalyst, that leaves the existing structures intact but merely facilitates new uses of these structures, and when, by contrast, does it totally transform the existing structures?

Unanswered questions need not leave one dissatisfied and disappointed. Quite the opposite, they can leave one energized and awakened to new possibilities, open to the promise that new probes will pay dividends. Progress in the sciences consists every bit as much of asking a new set of questions as of answering old questions. Some of the most baffling questions are never answered. They are merely outgrown––by raising a new order of questions. It is the tantalizing blessing of new paradigms that they raise new questions. In this I have indulged in the present book while, I hope, providing some basis for taking the new questions seriously.

Of this I am convinced: Immediacy has its own special message. It can speak to us, if we have the wisdom to listen.

Index